Cynthia Wakeham's Money

by

Anna Katharine Green

Cynthia Wakeham's Money
by Anna Katharine Green

Copyright © 2023

All Rights reserved.

ISBN: 978-93-58711-12-7

Published by

DOUBLE 9 BOOKS

2/13-B, Ansari Road
Daryaganj, New Delhi – 110002
info@double9books.com
www.double9books.com
Tel. 011-40042856

ABOUT THE AUTHOR

The American author Anna Katharine Green (1846–1955), who is recognized as one of the forerunners of detective fiction, was raised in a sophisticated and educated household and was born in Brooklyn, New York. Her debut book, "The Leavenworth Case," which was released in 1878, quickly rose to popularity. She produced countless short pieces in the genre in addition to almost 40 books. Intricate riddles, brilliant storytelling, and the use of forensic evidence were hallmarks of her books, which also often included characters like detective Ebenezer Gryce and the single sleuth Amelia Butterworth. Along with her contributions to the genre, Green pioneered the exploration of gender and social class issues in mysteries, often utilizing her characters to remark on societal injustices. She was on the executive committee of the New York State Suffrage Association and sponsored issues including public health and education, demonstrating her commitment to women's suffrage and charity. Her contributions to the detective fiction genre are still respected and recognized in modern times.

CONTENTS

BOOK I.
A VILLAGE MYSTERY.

I.
A WOMAN'S FACE.

It was verging towards seven o'clock. The train had just left Marston station, and two young men stood on the platform surveying with very different eyes the stretch of country landscape lying before them. Frank Etheridge wore an eager aspect, the aspect of the bright, hopeful, energetic lawyer which he was, and his quick searching gaze flashed rapidly from point to point as if in one of the scattered homes within his view he sought an answer to some problem at present agitating his mind. He was a stranger in Marston.

His companion, Edgar Sellick, wore a quieter air, or at least one more restrained. He was a native of the place, and was returning to it after a short and fruitless absence in the west, to resume his career of physician amid the scenes of his earliest associations. Both were tall, well-made, and handsome, and, to draw at once a distinction between them which will effectually separate their personalities, Frank Etheridge was a man to attract the attention of men, and Edgar Sellick that of women; the former betraying at first glance all his good qualities in the keenness of his eye and the frankness of his smile, and the latter hiding his best impulses under an air of cynicism so allied to melancholy that imagination was allowed free play in his behalf. They had attended the same college and had met on the train by chance.

"I am expecting old Jerry, with a buggy," announced Edgar, looking indifferently down the road. The train was on time but Jerry was not, both of which facts were to be expected. "Ah, here he comes. You will ride to the tavern with me?"

"With pleasure," was Frank's cheerful reply; "but what will you do with Jerry? He's a mile too large, as you see yourself, to be a third party in a buggy ride."

"No doubt about that, but Jerry can walk; it will help to rob him of a little of his avoirdupois. As his future physician I shall prescribe it. I cannot have you miss the supper I have telegraphed for at Henly's."

And being a determined man, he carried this scheme through, to Jerry's manifest but cheerfully accepted discomfort. As they were riding off, Edgar leaned from the buggy, and Frank heard him say to his panting follower:

"Is it known in town that I am coming to-night?" To which that panting follower shrilly replied: "Ay, sir, and Tim Jones has lit a bond-fire and Jack Skelton hoisted a flag, so glad they be to have you back. Old Dudgeon was too intimate with the undertaker, sir. We hopes as you will turn a cold shoulder to him—the undertaker, I mean."

At which Frank observed his friend give one of his peculiar smiles which might mean so little and might mean so much, but whatever it meant had that touch of bittersweet in it which at once hurts and attracts.

"You like your profession?" Frank abruptly asked.

Edgar turned, surveyed the other questioningly for a moment, then remarked:

"Not as you like yours. Law seems to be a passion with you."

Frank laughed. "Why not? I have no other love, why not give all my heart to that?"

Edgar did not answer; he was looking straight before him at the lights in the village they were now rapidly approaching.

"How strange it is we should have met in this way," exclaimed the young lawyer. "It is mighty fortunate for me, whatever it may be for you. You know all the people in town, and perhaps can tell me what will shorten my stay into hours."

"Do you call that fortunate?" interrogated the other with one of his quiet smiles.

"Well, no, only from a business view. But you see, Edgar, it is so short a time since I have thought of anything but business, that I have hardly got used to the situation. I should be sorry, now I come to think of it, to say good-by to you before I heard how you had enjoyed life since we parted on a certain Commencement day. You look older, while I——"

He laughed. How merry the sound, and how the growing twilight seemed to brighten at it! Edgar looked for a moment as if he envied him that laugh, then he said:

"You are not tripped up by petty obstacles. You have wings to your feet and soar above small disappointments. My soles cling to the ground and encounter there difficulty after difficulty. Hence the weariness with which I gain anything. But your business here,—what is it? You say I can aid you. How?"

"Oh, it is a long story which will help to enliven our evening meal. Let us wait till then. At present I am interested in what I see before me. Snug homes, Edgar, and an exquisite landscape."

The other, whose face for the last few minutes had been gradually settling into sterner and sterner lines, nodded automatically but did not look up from the horse he was driving.

"Who lives in these houses? Old friends of yours?" Frank continued.

Edgar nodded again, whipped his horse and for an instant allowed his eyes to wander up and down the road.

"I used to know them all," he acknowledged, "but I suppose there have been changes."

His tone had altered, his very frame had stiffened. Frank looked at him curiously.

"You seem to be in a hurry," he remarked. "I enjoy this twilight drive, and—haloo! this is an odd old place we are coming to. Suppose you pull up and let me look at it."

His companion, with a strange glance and an awkward air of dissatisfaction, did as he was bid, and Frank leaning from the buggy gazed long and earnestly at the quaint old house and grounds which had attracted his attention. Edgar did not follow his example but sat unmoved, looking fixedly at the last narrow strip of orange light that separated night from day on the distant horizon.

"I feel as if I had come upon something uncanny," murmured Frank. "Look at that double row of poplars stretching away almost as far as we can see? Is it not an ideal Ghost's Walk, especially in this hour of falling shadows. I never saw anything so suggestive in a country landscape before. Each tree looks like a spectre hob-nobbing with its neighbor. Tell me that this is a haunted house which guards this avenue. Nothing less weird should dominate a spot so peculiar."

"Frank, I did not know you were so fanciful," exclaimed the other, lashing his horse with a stinging whip.

"Wait, wait! I am not fanciful, it is the place that is curious. If you were not in a hurry for your supper you would see it too. Come, give it a look.

You may have observed it a hundred times before, but by this light you must acknowledge that it looks like a place with a history. Come, now, don't it?"

Edgar drew in his horse for the second time and impatiently allowed his glance to follow in the direction indicated by his friend. What he saw has already been partially described. But details will not be amiss here, as the house and its surroundings were really unique, and bespoke an antiquity of which few dwellings can now boast even in the most historic parts of Connecticut.

The avenue of poplars which had first attracted Frank's attention had this notable peculiarity, that it led from nowhere to nowhere. That is, it was not, as is usual in such cases, made the means of approach to the house, but on the contrary ran along its side from road to rear, thick, compact, and gruesome. The house itself was of timber, and was both gray and weather-beaten. It was one of the remnants of that old time when a family homestead rambled in all directions under a huge roof which accommodated itself to each new projection, like the bark to its tree. In this case the roof sloped nearly to the ground on one side, while on the other it beetled over a vine-clad piazza. In front of the house and on both sides of it rose a brick wall that, including the two rows of trees within its jealous cordon, shut off the entire premises from those of the adjoining neighbors, and gave to the whole place an air of desolation and remoteness which the smoke rising from its one tall chimney did not seem to soften or relieve. Yet old as it all was, there was no air of decay about the spot, nor was the garden neglected or the vines left untrimmed.

"The home of a hermit," quoth Frank. "You know who lives there of course, but if you did not I would wager that it is some old scion of the past—
—"

Suddenly he stopped, suddenly his hand was laid on the horse's rein falling somewhat slack in the grasp of his companion. A lamp had at that instant been brought into one of the front rooms of the house he was contemplating, and the glimpse he thus caught of the interior attracted his eyes and even arrested the gaze of the impatient Edgar. For the woman who held the lamp was no common one, and the face which showed above it was one to stop any man who had an eye for the beautiful, the inscrutable, and the tragic. As Frank noted it and marked its exquisite lines, its faultless coloring, and that air of profound and mysterious melancholy which made it stand out distinctly in the well-lighted space about it, he tightened his grip on the reins he had snatched, till the horse stood still in the road, and Edgar impatiently watching him, perceived that the gay look had crept from his face, leaving there an expression of indefinable yearning which at once transfigured and ennobled it.

"What beauty! What unexpected beauty!" Frank whispered at last. "Did you ever see its like, Edgar?"

The answer came with Edgar's most cynical smile:

"Wait till she turns her head."

And at that moment she did turn it. On the instant Frank drew in his breath and Edgar expected to see him drop his hand from the reins and sink back disillusionized and indifferent. But he did not. On the contrary, his attitude betrayed a still deeper interest and longing, and murmuring, "How sad! poor girl!" he continued to gaze till Edgar, with one strange, almost shrinking look in the direction of the unconscious girl now moving abstractedly across the room, tore the reins from his hands and started the horse again towards their place of destination.

Frank, whom the sudden movement seemed to awaken as from a dream, glanced for a moment almost angrily at his companion, then he settled back in his seat, saying nothing till the lights of the tavern became visible, when he roused himself and inquired:

"Who is that girl, Edgar, and how did she become so disfigured?"

"I don't know," was the short reply; "she has always been so, I believe, at least since I remember seeing her. It looks like the scar of a wound, but I have never heard any explanation given of it."

"Her name, Edgar?"

"Hermione Cavanagh."

"You know her?"

"Somewhat."

"Are you"—the words came with a pant, shortly, intensely, and as if forced from him—"in love—with her?"

"No." Edgar's passion seemed for the moment to be as great as that of the other. "How came you to think of such a thing?"

"Because—because," Frank whispered almost humbly, "you seemed so short in your replies, and because, I might as well avow it, she seems to me one to command the love of all men."

"Well, sirs, here I be as quick as you," shouted a voice in their rear, and old Jerry came lumbering forward, just in time to hold their horse as they alighted at the tavern.

II.
A LAWYER'S ADVENTURE.

Supper that night did not bring to these two friends all the enjoyment which they had evidently anticipated. In the first place it was continually interrupted by greetings to the young physician whose unexpected return to his native town had awakened in all classes a decided enthusiasm. Then Frank was moody, he who was usually gaiety itself. He wanted to talk about the beautiful and unfortunate Miss Cavanagh, and Edgar did not, and this created embarrassment between them, an embarrassment all the more marked that there seemed to be some undefined reason for Edgar's reticence not to be explained by any obvious cause. At length Frank broke out impetuously:

"If you won't tell me anything about this girl, I must look up some one who will. Those cruel marks on her face have completed the charm of her beauty, and not till I know something of their history and of her, will I go to sleep to-night. So much for the impression which a woman's face can make upon an unsusceptible man."

"Frank," observed the other, coldly, "I should say that your time might be much better employed in relating to me the cause for your being in Marston."

The young lawyer started, shook himself, and laughed.

"Oh, true, I had forgotten," said he, and supper being now over he got up and began pacing the floor. "Do you know any one here by the name of Harriet Smith?"

"No," returned the other, "but I have been away a year, and many persons may have come into town in that time."

"But I mean an old resident," Frank explained, "a lady of years, possibly a widow."

"I never heard of such a person," rejoined Edgar. "Are you sure there is such a woman in town? I should be apt to know it if there were."

"I am not sure she is here now, or for that matter that she is living, but if she is not and I learn the names and whereabouts of any heirs she may have left behind her, I shall be satisfied with the results of my journey. Harriet Smith! Surely you have heard of her."

"No," Edgar protested, "I have not."

"It is odd," remarked Frank, wrinkling his brows in some perplexity. "I thought I should have no trouble in tracing her. Not that I care," he avowed with brightening countenance. "On the contrary, I can scarcely quarrel with a fact that promises to detain me in your company for a few days."

"No? Then your mind has suddenly changed in that regard," Edgar dryly insinuated.

Frank blushed. "I think not," was his laughing reply. "But let me tell my story. It may interest you in a pursuit that I begin to see is likely to possess difficulties." And lighting a cigar, he sat down with his friend by the open window. "I do not suppose you know much about Brooklyn, or, if you do, that you are acquainted with that portion of it which is called Flatbush. I will therefore explain that this outlying village is a very old one, antedating the Revolution. Though within a short car-drive from the great city, it has not yet given up its life to it, but preserves in its one main street at least, a certain individuality which still connects it with the past. My office, as you know, is in New York, but I have several clients in Brooklyn and one or two in Flatbush, so I was not at all surprised, though considerably put out, when one evening, just as I was about to start for the theatre, a telegram was handed me by the janitor, enjoining me to come without delay to Flatbush prepared to draw up the will of one, Cynthia Wakeham, lying, as the sender of the telegram declared, at the point of death. Though I knew neither this name, nor that of the man who signed it, which was Hiram Huckins, and had no particular desire to change the place of my destination at that hour, I had really no good reason for declining the business thus offered me. So making a virtue of necessity, I gave up the theatre and started instead for Flatbush, which, from the house where I lodge in upper New York, is a good hour and a half's ride even by the way of the bridge and the elevated roads. It was therefore well on towards ten o'clock before I arrived in the shaded street which in the daylight and in the full brightness of a summer's sun I had usually found so attractive, but which at night and under the circumstances which had brought me there looked both sombre and forbidding. However I had not come upon an errand of pleasure, so I did not spend much time in contemplating my surroundings, but beckoning to the conductor of the street-car on which I was riding, I asked him if he knew Mrs. Wakeham's house, and when he nodded, asked him to set me down before it. I thought he gave me a queer look, but as his attention was at that moment diverted, I could not be sure of it, and before he came my way again the car had stopped and he was motioning to me to alight.

"'That is the house,' said he, pointing to two huge gate-posts glimmering whitely in the light of a street-lamp opposite, and I was on the sidewalk and in front of the two posts before I remembered that a man on the rear platform of the car had muttered as I stepped by him: 'A visitor for Widow Wakeham, eh; she *must* be sick, then!'

"The house stood back a short distance from the street, and as I entered the gate, which by the way looked as if it would tumble down if I touched it, I could see nothing but a gray mass with one twinkling light in it. But as I drew nearer I became aware that it was not a well-kept and hospitable mansion towards which I was tending, however imposing might be its size and general structure. If only from the tangled growth of the shrubbery about me and the long dank stalks of the weeds that lay as if undisturbed by mortal feet upon the walk, I could gather that whatever fortune Mrs. Wakeham might have to leave she had not expended much in the keeping of her home. But it was upon reaching the house I experienced the greatest surprise. There were walls before me, no doubt, and a huge portico, but the latter was hanging as it were by faith to supports so dilapidated that even the darkness of that late hour could not hide their ruin or the impending fall of the whole structure. So old, so uncared-for, and so utterly out of keeping with the errand upon which I had come looked the whole place that I instinctively drew back, assured that the conductor had made some mistake in directing me thither. But no sooner had I turned my back upon the house, than a window was thrown up over my head and I heard the strangely eager voice of a man say:

"'This is the place, sir. Wait, and I will open the door for you.'

"I did as he bade me, though not without some reluctance. The voice, for all its tone of anxiety, sounded at once false and harsh, and I instinctively associated with it a harsh and false face. The house, too, did not improve in appearance upon approach. The steps shook under my tread, and I could not but notice by the faint light sifting through the bushes from the lamp on the other side of the way, that the balustrades had been pulled from their places, leaving only gaping holes to mark where they had once been. The door was intact, but in running my hand over it I discovered that the mouldings had been stripped from its face, and that the knocker, hanging as it did by one nail, was ready to fall at the first provocation. If Cynthia Wakeham lived here, it would be interesting to know the extent of her wealth. As there seemed to be some delay in the opening of the door, I had time to note that the grounds (all of these houses have grounds about them) were of some extent, but, as I have said, in a manifest condition of overgrowth and neglect. As I mused upon the contrast they must afford in the bright daylight to the wide and well-kept lawns of the more ambitious owners on either side, a footstep sounded on the loose boards which had evidently been flung down at one side of the house as a sort of protection to the foot from the darkness and mud of the neglected path, and a woman's form swung dimly into view, laden with a great pile of what looked to me like brushwood. As she passed she seemed to become conscious of my presence, and, looking up, she let the huge bundle slip slowly from her shoulders till it lay in the darkness at her feet.

"'Are you,' she whispered, coming close to the foot of the steps, 'going in there?'

"'Yes,' I returned, struck by the mingled surprise and incredulity in her tone.

"She stood still a minute, then came up a step.

"'Are you a minister?' she asked.

"'No,' I laughed; 'why?'

"She seemed to reason with herself before saying: 'No one ever goes into that house; I thought perhaps you did not know. They won't have any one. Would you mind telling me,' she went on, in a hungry whisper almost thrilling to hear, coming as it did through the silence and darkness of the night, 'what you find in the house? I will be at the gate, sir, and — —'

"She paused, probably awed by the force of my exclamation, and picking up her bundle of wet boughs, slunk away, but not without turning more than once before she reached the gate. Scarcely had she disappeared into the street when a window went up in a neighboring house. At the same moment, some one, I could not tell whether it was a man or a woman, came up the path as far as the first trees and there paused, while a shrill voice called out:

"'They never unlocks that door; visitors ain't wanted.'

"Evidently, if I were not admitted soon I should have the whole neighborhood about me.

"I lifted the knocker, but it came off in my hand. Angry at the mischance, and perhaps a little moved by the excitement of my position, I raised the broken piece of iron and gave a thundering knock on the rotten panels before me. Instantly the door opened, creaking ominously as it did so, and a man stood in the gap with a wretched old kerosene lamp in his hand. The apologetic leer on his evil countenance did not for a moment deceive me.

"'I beg your pardon,' he hurriedly exclaimed, and his voice showed he was a man of education, notwithstanding his forlorn and wretched appearance, 'but the old woman had a turn just as you came, and I could not leave her.'

"I looked at him, and instinct told me to quit the spot and not enter a house so vilely guarded. For the man was not only uncouth to the last degree in dress and aspect, but sinister in expression and servilely eager in bearing.

"'Won't you come in?' he urged. 'The old woman is past talking, but she can make signs; perhaps an hour from now she will not be able to do even that.'

"'Do you allude to the woman who wishes to make her will?' I asked.

"'Yes,' he answered, greedily, 'Cynthia Wakeham, my sister.' And he gently pushed the door in a way that forced me to enter or show myself a coward.

"I took heart and went in. What poverty I beheld before me in the light of that solitary smoking lamp! If the exterior of the house bore the marks of devastation, what shall I say of the barren halls and denuded rooms which now opened before me? Not a chair greeted my eyes, though a toppling stool here and there showed that people sat in this place. Nor did I see a table, though somewhere in some remote region beyond the staircase I heard the clatter of plates, as if eating were also known in this home of almost ostentatious penury. Staircase I say, but I should have said steps, for the balustrades were missing here just as they had been missing without, and not even a rail remained to speak of old-time comfort and prosperity.

"'I am very poor,' humbly remarked the man, answering my look of perplexity. 'It is my sister who has the money.' And moving towards the stairs, he motioned me to ascend.

"Even then I recoiled, not knowing what to make of this adventure; but hearing a hollow groan from above, uttered in tones unmistakably feminine, I remembered my errand and went up, followed so closely by the man, that his breath, mingled with the smell of that vile lamp, seemed to pant on my shoulder. I shall never smell kerosene again without recalling the sensations of that moment.

"Arriving at the top of the stair, up which my distorted shadow had gone before me, I saw an open door and went in. A woman was lying in one corner on a hard and uncomfortable bed, a woman whose eyes drew me to her side before a word had been spoken.

"She was old and in the last gasp of some fatal disease. But it was not this which impressed me most. It was the searching look with which she greeted me,—a piteous, hunted look, like that of some wild animal driven to bay and turning upon her conqueror for some signs of relenting or pity. It made the haggard face eloquent; it assured me without a word that some great wrong had been done or was about to be done, and that I must show myself at once her friend if I would gain her confidence.

"Advancing to her side, I spoke to her kindly, asking if she were Cynthia Wakeham, and if she desired the services of a lawyer.

"She at once nodded painfully but unmistakably, and, lifting her hand, pointed to her lips and shook her head.

"'She means that she cannot speak', explained the man, in a pant, over my shoulder.

"Moving a step aside in my disgust, I said to her, not to him:

"'But you can hear?'

"Her intelligent eye responded before her head could add its painful acquiescence.

"'And you have property to leave?'

"'This house', answered the man.

"My eyes wandered mechanically to the empty cupboards about me from which the doors had been wrenched and, as I now saw from the looks of the fireplace, burned.

"'The ground—the ground is worth something,' quoth the man.

"'The avidity with which he spoke satisfied me at least upon one point— *he* was the expectant heir.

"'Your name?' I asked, turning sharply upon him.

"'Hiram Huckins.'

"It was the name attached to the telegram.

"'And you are the brother of this woman?'

"'Yes, yes.'

"I had addressed him, but I looked at her. She answered my look with a steadfast gaze, but there was no dissent in it, and I considered that point settled.

"'She is a married woman, then?'

"'A widow; husband died long years ago.'

"'Any children?'

"'No.' And I saw in her face that he spoke the truth.

"'But you and she have brothers or sisters? You are not her only relative?'

"'I am the only one who has stuck by her,' he sullenly answered. 'We did have a sister, but she is gone; fled from home years ago; lost in the great world; dead, perhaps. *She* don't care for her; ask her.'

"I did ask her, but the haggard face said nothing. The eyes burned, but they had a waiting look.

"'To whom do you want to leave your property?' I inquired of her pointedly.

"Had she glanced at the man, had her face even changed, or so much as a tremor shook her rigid form, I might have hesitated. But the quiet way in which she lifted her hand and pointed with one finger in his direction while she looked straight at me, convinced me that whatever was wrong, her mind was made up as to the disposal of her property. So taking out my papers, I sat down on the rude bench drawn up beside the bed and began to write.

"The man stood behind me with the lamp. He was so eager and bent over me so closely that the smell of the lamp and his nearness were more than I could bear.

"'Set down the lamp,' I cried. 'Get a table—something—don't lean over me like that.'

"But there was nothing, actually nothing for him to put the lamp on, and I was forced to subdue my disgust and get used as best I could to his presence and to his great shadow looming on the wall behind us. But I could not get used to her eyes hurrying me, and my hand trembled as I wrote.

"'Have you any name but Cynthia?' I inquired, looking up.

"She painfully shook her head.

"'You had better tell me what her husband's name was,' I suggested to the brother.

"'John Lapham Wakeham,' was the quick reply.

"I wrote down both names. Then I said, looking intently at the dying widow:

"'As you cannot speak, you must make signs. Shake your hand when you wish to say no, and move it up and down when you wish to say yes. Do you understand?'

"She signalled somewhat impatiently that she did, and then, lifting her hand with a tremulous movement, pointed anxiously towards a large Dutch clock, which was the sole object of adornment in the room.

"'She urges you to hurry,' whispered the man. 'Make it short, make it short. The doctor I called in this morning said she might die any minute.'

"As from her appearance I judged this to be only too possible, I hastily wrote a few words more, and then asked:

"'Is this property all that you have to leave?'

"I had looked at her, though I knew it would be the man who would answer.

"'Yes, yes, this house,' he cried. 'Put it strong; this house and all there is in it.'

"I thought of its barren rooms and empty cupboards, and a strange fancy seized me. Going straight to the woman, I leaned over her and said:

"'Is it your desire to leave all that you possess to this brother? Real property and personal, this house, and also everything it contains?'

"She did not answer, even by a sign, but pointed again to the clock.

"'She means that you are to go right on,' he cried. 'And indeed you must,' he pursued, eagerly. 'She won't be able to sign her name if you wait much longer.'

"I felt the truth of this, and yet I hesitated.

"'Where are the witnesses?' I asked. 'She must have two witnesses to her signature.'

"'Won't I do for one?' he inquired.

"'No,' I returned; 'the one benefited by a will is disqualified from witnessing it.'

"He looked confounded for a moment. Then he stepped to the door and shouted, 'Briggs! Briggs!'

"As if in answer there came a clatter as of falling dishes, and as proof of the slavery which this woman had evidently been under to his avarice, she gave a start, dying as she was, and turned upon him with a frightened gaze, as if she expected from him an ebullition of wrath.

"'Briggs, is there a light in Mr. Thompson's house?'

"'Yes,' answered a gruff voice from the foot of the stairs.

"'Go then, and ask him or the first person you see there, if he will come in here for a minute. Be very polite and don't swear, or I won't pay you the money I promised you. Say that Mrs. Wakeham is dying, and that the lawyer is drawing up her will. Get James Sotherby to come too, and if he won't do it, somebody else who is respectable. Everything must be very legal, sir,' he explained, turning to me, 'very legal.'

"Not knowing what to think of this man, but seeing only one thing to do, I nodded, and asked the woman whom I should name as executor. She at once indicated her brother, and as I wrote in his name and concluded the will, she watched me with an intentness that made my nerves creep, though I am usually anything but susceptible to such influences. When the document was ready I rose and stood at her side in some doubt of the whole transaction. Was it her will I had expressed in the paper I held before me, or his? Had she been constrained by his influence to do what she was doing, or was her mind free to act and but obeying its natural instincts? I determined to make one effort at finding out. Turning towards the man, I said firmly:

"'Before Mrs. Wakeham signs this will she must know exactly what it contains. I can read it to her, but I prefer her to read the paper for herself. Get her glasses, then, if she needs them, and bring them here at once, or I throw up this business and take the document away with me out of the house.'

"'But she has no glasses,' he protested; 'they were broken long ago.'

"'Get them,' I cried; 'or get yours,—she shall not sign that document till you do.'

"But he stood hesitating, loth, as I now believe, to leave us together, though that was exactly what I desired, which she, seeing, feverishly clutched my sleeve, and, with a force of which I should not have thought her capable, made wild gestures to the effect that I should not delay any longer, but read it to her myself.

"Seeing by this, as I thought, that her own feelings were, notwithstanding my doubts, really engaged in the same direction as his, I desisted from my efforts to separate the two, if it were only for a moment, and read the will aloud. It ran thus:

"The last will and testament of Cynthia Wakeham, widow of John Lapham Wakeham, of Flatbush, Kings County, New York.

"First: I direct all my just debts and funeral expenses to be paid.

"Second: I give, devise, and bequeath to my brother, Hiram Huckins, all the property, real and personal, which I own, or to which I may be entitled, at the time of my death, and I appoint him the sole executor of this my last will and testament.

"Witness my hand this fifth day of June, in the year eighteen hundred and eighty-eight.

"Signed, published, and declared by the Testatrix to be her last will and testament, in our presence who, at her request and in her presence and in the presence of each other, have subscribed our names hereto as witnesses, on this 5th day of June, 1888.

"'Is that the expression of your wishes?' I asked, when I had finished.

"She nodded, and reached out her hand for the pen.

"'You must wait,' said I, 'for the witnesses.'

"But even as I spoke their approach was heard, and Huckins was forced to go to the door with the lamp, for the hall was pitch dark and the stairs dangerous. As he turned his back upon us, I thought Mrs. Wakeham moved and opened her lips, but I may have been mistaken, for his black and ominous shadow lay over her face, and I could discern but little of its expression.

"'Is there anything you want?' I asked her, rising and going to the bedside.

"But Huckins was alert to all my movements, if he had stepped for a moment away.

"'Give her water,' he cried, wheeling sharply about. And pointing to a broken glass standing on the floor at her side, he watched me while I handed it to her.

"'She mus'n't give out now,' he pursued, with one eye on us and the other on the persons coming upstairs.

"'She will not,' I returned, seeing her face brighten at the sound of approaching steps.

"'It's Miss Thompson and Mr. Dickey,' now spoke up the gruff voice of Briggs from the foot of the steps. 'No other folks was up, so I brought them along.'

"The young woman, who at this instant appeared in the doorway, blushed and cast a shy look over her shoulder at the fresh-faced man who followed her.

"'It's all right, Minnie,' immediately interposed that genial personage, with a cheerful smile; 'every one knows we are keeping company and mean to be married as soon as the times improve.'

"'Yes, every one knows,' she sighed, and stepped briskly into the room, her intelligent face and kindly expression diffusing a cheer about her such as the dismal spot had doubtless lacked for years.

"I heard afterward that this interesting couple had been waiting for the times to improve, for the last fifteen years."

III.
CONTINUATION OF A LAWYER'S ADVENTURE.

"Thetwo witnesses had scarcely entered the room before the dying woman stretched out her hand again for the pen. As I handed it to her and placed the document before her on my portfolio, I asked:

"'Do you declare this paper to be your last will and testament and do you request these persons to witness it?'

"She bowed a quick acquiescence, and put the pen at the place I pointed out to her.

"'Shall I support your hand?' I pursued, fearful she would not have the strength to complete the task.

"But she shook her head and wrote her name in hastily, with a feverish energy that astonished me. Expecting to see her drop back exhausted if not lifeless as the pen left the paper, I drew the document away and bent to support her. But she did not need my assistance. Indeed she looked stronger than before, and what was still more astonishing, seemed even more anxious and burningly eager.

"'Is she holding up till the witnesses have affixed their signatures?' I inwardly queried. And intent upon relieving her, I hastily explained to them the requirements of the case, and did not myself breathe easily till I saw their two names below hers. Then I felt that she could rest; but to my surprise but one sigh of relief rose in that room, and that was from the cringing, cruel-eyed inheritor, who, at the first intimation that the document was duly signed and attested, sprang from his corner with such a smile that the place seemed to grow hideous, and I drew involuntarily back.

"'Let me have it,' were his first words. 'I have lived in this hole, and for fifteen years made myself a slave to her whims, till I have almost rotted away like the place itself. And now I want my reward. Let me have the will.'

"His hand was on the paper and in my surprise I had almost yielded it up to him, when another hand seized it, and the dying, gasping woman, mumbling and mouthing, pointed for the third time to the clock and then to one corner of the paper, trying to make me understand something I entirely failed to comprehend.

"'What is it?' I asked. 'What do you want? Is not the will to your liking?'

"'Yes, yes,' her frenzied nods seemed to say, and yet she continued pointing to the clock and then to the paper while the angry man before her stared and muttered in a mixture of perplexity and alarm which added no little to the excitement of the harrowing scene.

"'Let me see if I can tell what she wants,' suddenly observed the young woman who had signed the paper as a witness. And bringing her sweet womanly face around where the rolling eye of the woman could see her, she asked with friendly interest in her tone, 'Do you wish the time of day written on the will?'

"Oh, the relief that swept over that poor woman's tortured countenance! She nodded and looked up at me so confidingly that in despite of the oddity of the request I rapidly penned after the date, the words 'at half-past ten o'clockP.M.,' and caused the witnesses to note the addition.

"This seemed to satisfy her, and she sank back with a sign that I was to yield to her brother's demand and give him the paper he coveted, and when I hesitated, started up again with such a frenzied appeal in her face that in the terror of seeing her die before our eyes, I yielded it to his outstretched hand, expecting at the most to see him put it in his pocket.

"But no, the moment he felt it in his grasp, he set down the lamp, and, without a look in her direction or a word of thanks to me or the two neighbors who had come to his assistance, started rapidly from the room. Disturbed and doubting my own wisdom in thus yielding to an impulse of humanity which may be called weakness by such strong-minded men as yourself, I turned to follow him, but the woman's trembling hand again stopped me; and convinced at last that I was alarming myself unnecessarily and that she had had as much pleasure in making him her heir as he in being made so, I turned to pay her my adieux, when the expression of her face, changed now from what it had been to one of hope and trembling delight, made me pause again in wonder, and almost prepared me for the low and thrilling whisper which now broke from her lips in distinct tones.

"'Is he gone?'

"'Then you can speak,' burst from the young woman.

"The widow gave her an eloquent look.

"'I have not spoken,' said she, 'for two days; I have been saving my strength. Hark!' she suddenly whispered. 'He has no light, he will pitch over the landing. No, no, he has gone by it in safety, he has reached——' she paused and listened intently, trembling as she did so—'Will he go into *that* room?—Run! follow! see if he has dared—but no, he has gone down to the kitchen,' came in quick glad relief from her lips as a distant door shut softly at the back end of the house. 'He is leaving the house and will never come back. I am released forever from his watchfulness; I am free! Now, sir, draw up another will, quick; let these two kind friends wait and see me sign it, and God will bless you for your kindness and my eyes will close in peace upon this cruel world.'

"Aghast but realizing in a moment that she had but lent herself to her brother's wishes in order to rid herself of a surveillance which had possibly had an almost mesmeric influence upon her, I opened my portfolio again, saying:

"'You declare yourself then to have been unduly influenced by your brother in making the will you have just signed in the presence of these two witnesses?'

"To which she replied with every evidence of a clear mind——

"'I do; I do. I could not move, I could not breathe, I could not think except as he willed it. When he was near, and he was always near, I had to do just as he wished—perhaps because I was afraid of him, perhaps because he had the stronger will of the two, I do not know; I cannot explain it, but he ruled me and has done so all my life till this hour. Now he has left me, left me to die, as he thinks, unfriended and alone, but I am strong yet, stronger than he knows, and before I turn my face to the wall, I will tear my property from his unholy grasp and give it where I have always wanted it to go—to my poor, lost, unfortunate sister.'

"'Ah,' thought I, 'I see, I see'; and satisfied at last that I was no longer being made the minister of an unscrupulous avarice, I hastily drew up a second will, only pausing to ask the name of her sister and the place of her residence.

"'Her name is Harriet Smith,' was the quick reply, 'and she lived when last I heard of her in Marston, a little village in Connecticut. She may be dead now, it is so long since I received any news of her,—Hiram would never let me write to her,—but she may have had children, and if so, they are just as welcome as she is to the little I have to give.'

"'Her children's names?' I asked.

"'I don't know, I don't know anything about her. But you will find out everything necessary when I am gone; and if she is living, or has children, you will see that they are reinstated in the home of their ancestors. For,' she now added eagerly, 'they must come here to live, and build up this old house again and make it respectable once more or they cannot have my money. I want you to put that in my will; for when I have seen these old walls toppling, the doors wrenched off, and its lintels demolished for firewood, for *firewood*, sir, I have kept my patience alive and my hope up by saying, Never mind; some day Harriet's children will make this all right again. The old house which their kind grandfather was good enough to give me for my own, shall not fall to the ground without one effort on my part to save it. And this is how I will accomplish it. This house is for Harriet or Harriet's children if they will come here and live in it one year, but if they will not do this, let it go to my brother, for I shall have no more interest in it. You heed me, lawyer?'

"I nodded and wrote on busily, thinking, perhaps, that if Harriet or Harriet's children did not have some money of their own to fix up this old place, they would scarcely care to accept their forlorn inheritance. Meantime the two witnesses who had lingered at the woman's whispered entreaty exchanged glances, and now and then a word expressive of the interest they were taking in this unusual affair.

"'Who is to be the executor of *this* will?' I inquired.

"'You,' she cried. Then, as I started in surprise, she added: 'I know nobody but you. Put yourself in as executor, and oh, sir, when it is all in your hands, find my lost relatives, I beseech you, and bring them here, and take them into my mother's room at the end of the hall, and tell them it is all theirs, and that they must make it their room and fix it up and lay a new floor—you remember, a new floor—and——' Her words rambled off incoherently, but her eyes remained fixed and eager.

"I wrote in my name as executor.

"When the document was finished, I placed it before her and asked the young lady who had been acting as my lamp-bearer to read it aloud. This she did; the second will reading thus:

"The last will and testament of Cynthia Wakeham, widow of
John Lapham Wakeham, of Flatbush, Kings County, New York.

"First: I direct all my just debts and funeral expenses to be paid.

"Second: I give, devise, and bequeath all my property to my sister, Harriet Smith, if living at my death, and, if not living, then to her children living at my death, in equal shares, upon condition, nevertheless, that the legatee or legatees who take under this will shall forthwith take up their residence in the house I now occupy in Flatbush, and continue to reside therein for at least one year thence next ensuing. If neither my said sister nor any of her descendants be living at my death, or if so living, the legatee who takes hereunder shall fail to comply with the above conditions, then all of said property shall go to my brother, Hiram Huckins.

"Third: I appoint Frank Etheridge, of New York City, sole executor of this my last will and testament, thereby revoking all other wills by me made, especially that which was executed on this date at half-past ten o'clock.

"Witness my hand this fifth day of June, in the year eighteen hundred and eighty-eight.

"Signed, published, and declared by the testatrix to be her last will and testament, in our presence, who, at her request and in her presence and in the presence of each other, have subscribed our names hereto as witnesses, on this 5th day of June, 1888, at five minutes to elevenP.M.

"This was satisfactory to the dying widow, and her strength kept up till she signed it and saw it duly attested; but when that was done, and the document safely stowed away in my pocket, she suddenly collapsed and sank back in a dying state upon her pillow.

"'What are we going to do?' now cried Miss Thompson, with looks of great compassion at the poor woman thus bereft, at the hour of death, of the natural care of relatives and friends. 'We cannot leave her here alone. Has she no doctor—no nurse?'

"'Doctors cost money,' murmured the almost speechless sufferer. And whether the smile which tortured her poor lips as she said these words was one of bitterness at the neglect she had suffered, or of satisfaction at the thought she had succeeded in saving this expense, I have never been able to decide.

"As I stooped to raise her now fallen head a quick, loud sound came to our ears from the back of the house, as of boards being ripped up from the floor by a reckless and determined hand. Instantly the woman's face assumed a ghastly look, and, tossing up her arms, she cried:

"'He has found the box!—the box! Stop him! Do not let him carry it away! It is — —' She fell back, and I thought all was over; but in another instant she had raised herself almost to a sitting position, and was pointing straight at the clock. 'There! there! look! the clock!' And without a sigh or another movement she sank back on the pillow, dead."

IV.
FLINT AND STEEL.

"Greatlystartled, I drew back from the bed which but a moment before had been the scene of such mingled emotions.

"'All is over here,' said I, and turned to follow the man whom with her latest breath she had bidden me to stop from leaving the house.

"As I could not take the lamp and leave my companions in darkness, I stepped out into a dark hall; but before I had taken a half dozen steps I heard a cautious foot descending the back stairs, and realizing that it would be both foolish and unsafe for me to endeavor to follow him through the unlighted rooms and possibly intricate passages of this upper hall, I bounded down the front stairs, and feeling my way from door to door, at last emerged into a room where there was a lamp burning.

"I had found the kitchen, and in it were Huckins and the man Briggs. Huckins had his hand on the latch of the outside door, and from his look and the bundle he carried, I judged that if I had been a minute later he would have been in full flight from the house.

"'Put out the light!' he shouted to Briggs.

"But I stepped forward, and the man did not dare obey him, and Huckins himself looked cowed and dropped his hand from the door-knob.

"'Where are you going?' I asked, moving rapidly to his side.

"'Isn't she dead?' was his only answer, given with a mixture of mockery and triumph difficult to describe.

"'Yes,' I assented, 'she is dead; but that does not justify you in flying the house.'

"'And who says I am flying?' he protested. 'Cannot I go out on an errand without being told I am running away?'

"'An errand,' I repeated, 'two minutes after your sister has breathed her last! Don't talk to me of errands. Your appearance is that of flight, and that bundle in your arms looks like the cause of it.'

"His eye, burning with a passion very natural under the circumstances, flashed over me with a look of disdain.

"'And what do you know of my appearance, and what is it to you if I carry or do not carry a bundle out of this house? Am I not master of everything here?'

"'No,' I cried boldly; then, thinking it might perhaps be wiser not to undeceive him as to his position till I had fully sounded his purposes, I added somewhat nonchalantly: 'that is, you are not master enough to take anything away that belonged to your sister. If you can prove to me that there is nothing in that bundle save what is yours and was yours before your sister died, well and good, you may go away with it and leave your poor dead sister to be cared for in her own house by strangers. But while I have the least suspicion that property of any nature belonging to this estate is hidden away under that roll of old clothes, you stop here if I have to appeal first to the strength of my arms and then to that of the law.'

"'But,' he quavered, 'it is mine—*mine*. I am but carrying away my own. Did you not draw up the will yourself? Don't you know she gave everything to me?'

"'What I know has nothing to do with it,' I retorted. 'Did you think because you saw a will drawn up in your favor that therefore you had immediate right to what she left, and could run away with her effects before her body was cold? A will has to be proven, my good man, before an heir has any right to touch what it leaves. If you do not know this, why did you try to slink away like a thief, instead of walking out of the front door like a proprietor? Your manner convicts you, man; so down with the bundle, or I shall have to give you in charge of the constable as a thief.'

"'You— —!' he began, but stopped. Either his fears were touched or his cunning awakened, for after surveying me for a moment with mingled doubt and hatred, he suddenly altered his manner, till it became almost cringing, and muttering consolingly to himself, 'After all it is only a delay; everything will soon be mine,' he laid the bundle on the one board of the broken table beside us, adding with hypocritical meekness: 'It was only some little keepsakes of my sister, not enough to make such a fuss about.'

"'I will see to these *keepsakes*,' said I, and was about to raise the bundle, when he sprang upon me.

"'You— —you— —!' he cried. 'What right have you to touch them or to look at them? Because you drew up the will, does that make you an authority here? I don't believe it, and I won't see you put on the airs of it. I will go for the constable myself. I am not afraid of the law. I will see who is master in this house where I have lived in wretched slavery for years, and of which I shall be soon the owner.'

"'Very well,' said I, 'let us go find the constable.'

"The calmness with which I uttered this seemed at once to abash and infuriate him.

"He alternately cringed and ruffled himself, shuffling from one foot to the other till I could scarcely conceal the disgust with which he inspired me. At last he blurted forth with forced bravado:

"'Have I any rights, or haven't I any rights! You think because I don't know the law, that you can make a fool of me, but you can't. I may have lived like a dog, and I may not have a good coat to my back, but I am the man to whom this property has been given, as no one knows better than yourself; and if I chose to lift my foot and kick you out of that door for calling me a thief, who would blame me?—answer me that.'

"'No one,' said I, with a serenity equal to his fury, 'if this property is indeed to be yours, and if I know it as you say.'

"Struck by the suggestion implied in these words, as by a blow in the face for which he was wholly unprepared, he recoiled for a moment, looking at me with mingled doubt and amazement.

"'And do you mean to deny to my face, within an hour of the fact, and with the very witnesses to it still in the house, what you yourself wrote in this paper I now flaunt in your face? If so, *you* are the fool, and I the cunning one, as you will yet see, Mr. Lawyer.'

"I met his look with great calmness.

"'The hour you speak of contained many minutes, Mr. Huckins; and it takes only a few for a woman to change her mind, and to record that change.'

"'Her mind?' The stare of terror and dismay in his eyes was contradicted by the laugh on his lips. 'What mind had she after I left her? She couldn't even speak. You cannot frighten me.'

"'Mr. Huckins,' I now said, beckoning to the two witnesses whom our loud talking had guided to the spot where we were, 'I have thought best to tell you what some men might have thought it more expedient perhaps to conceal. Mrs. Wakeham, who evidently felt herself unduly influenced by you in the making of that will you hold in your hand, immediately upon your withdrawal testified her desire to make another, and as I had no interest in the case save the desire to fulfil her real wishes, I at once complied with her request, and formally drew up a second will more in consonance with her evident desires.'

"'It is a lie, a lie; you are deceiving me!' shrieked the unhappy man, taken wholly by surprise. 'She couldn't utter a word; her tongue was paralyzed; how could you know her wishes?'

"'Mrs. Wakeham had some of the cunning of her brother,' I observed. 'She knew when to play dumb and when to speak. She talked very well when released from the influence of your presence.'

"Overwhelmed, he cast one glance at the two witnesses, who by this time had stepped to my side, and reading confirmation in the severity of their looks, he fell slowly back against the table where he stood leaning heavily, with his head fallen on his breast.

"'Who has she given the house to?' he asked at last faintly, almost humbly.

"'That I have no right to tell you,' I answered. 'When the will is offered for probate you will know; that is all the comfort I can give you.'

"'She has left nothing to me, that much I see,' he bitterly exclaimed; and his head, lifted with momentary passion, fell again. 'Ten years gone to the dogs,' he murmured; 'ten years, and not a cent in reward! It is enough to make a man mad.' Suddenly he started forward in irrepressible passion. 'You talk about influence,' he cried, 'my influence; what influence did *you* have upon her? Some, or she would never have dared to contradict her dying words in that way. But I'll have it out with you in the courts. I'll never submit to being robbed in this way.'

"'You do not know that you are robbed,' said I, 'wait till you hear the will.'

"'The will? This is her will!' he shrieked, waving before him the paper that he held; 'I will not believe in any other; I will not acknowledge any other.'

"'You may have to,' now spoke up Mr. Dickey in strong and hearty tones; 'and if I might advise you as a neighbor, I would say that the stiller you keep now the better it probably will be for you in the future. You have not earned a good enough reputation among us for disinterestedness to bluster in this way about your rights.'

"'I don't want any talk from you,' was Huckins' quick reply, but these words from one who had the ears of the community in which he lived had nevertheless produced their effect; for his manner changed and it was with quite a softened air that he finally put up the paper in his pocket and said: 'I beg pardon if I have talked too loud and passionately. But the property was given to me and it shall not be taken away if any fight on my part can keep it. So let me see you all go, for I presume you do not intend to take up your abode in this house just yet.'

"'No,' I retorted with some significance, 'though it might be worth our while. It may contain more keepsakes; I presume there are one or two boards yet that have not been ripped up from the floors.' Then ashamed of what was perhaps an unnecessary taunt, I hastened to add: 'My reason for telling you of the existence of a second will is that you might no longer make the one you hold an excuse for rifling these premises and abstracting their contents. Nothing here is yours—yet; and till you inherit, if ever you do inherit, any attempt to hide or carry away one article which is not manifestly your own, will be regarded by the law as a theft and will be punished as such. But,' I went on, seeking to still further mitigate language calculated to arouse any man's rage, whether he was a villain or not, 'you have too much sense, and doubtless too much honesty to carry out such intentions now you know that you have lost whatever rights you considered yourself to possess, so I will say no more about it but at once make my proposition, which is that we give this box into the charge of Mr. Dickey, who will stand surety for it till your sister can be found. If you agree to this——'

"'But I won't agree,' broke in Huckins, furiously. 'Do you think I am a fool? The box is mine, I say, and——'

"'Or perhaps,' I calmly interrupted, 'you would prefer the constable to come and take both it and the house in charge. This would better please me. Shall I send for the constable?'

"'No, no,——you! Do you want to make a prison-bird of me at once?'

"'I do not want to,' said I, 'but the circumstances force me to it. A house which has given up one treasure may give up another, and for this other I am accountable. Now as I cannot stay here myself to watch over the place, it necessarily follows that I must provide some one who can. And as an honest man you ought to desire this also. If you felt as I would under the circumstances, you would ask for the company of some disinterested person till our rival claims as executors had been duly settled and the right heir determined upon.'

"'But the constable? I don't want any constable.'

"'And you don't want Mr. Dickey?'

"'He's better than the constable.'

"'Very well; Mr. Dickey, will you stay?'

"'Yes, I'll stay; that's right, isn't it, Susan?'

"Miss Thompson who had been looking somewhat uneasy, brightened up as he spoke and answered cheerfully:

"'Yes, that's right. But who will see me home?'

"'Can you ask?' I inquired.

"She smiled and the matter was settled.

"In the hall I had the chance to whisper to Mr. Dickey:

"'Keep a sharp lookout on the fellow. I do not trust him, and he may be up to tricks. I will notify the constable of the situation and if you want help throw up a window and whistle. The man may make another attempt to rob the premises.'

"'That is so,' was the whispered reply. 'But he will have to play sharp to get ahead of me.'"

V.
DIFFICULTIES.

"Duringthe short walk that ensued we talked much of the dead widow and her sinister brother.

"'They belong to an old family,' observed Miss Thompson, 'and I have heard my mother tell how she has danced in their house at many a ball in the olden times. But ever since my day the place has borne evidences of decay, though it is only in the last five years it has looked as if it would fall to pieces. Which of them do you think was the real miser, he or she? Neither of them have had anything to do with their neighbors for ten years at least.'

"'Do not you know?' I asked.

"'No,' said she, 'and yet I have always lived in full view of their house. You see there were years in which no one lived there. Mr. Wakeham, who married this woman about the time father married mother, was a great invalid, and it was not till his death that the widow came back here to live. The father, who was a stern old man, I have heard mother tell, gave his property to her because she was the only one of his children who had not displeased him, but when she was a widow this brother came back to live with her, or on her, we have never been able to determine which. I think from what I have seen to-night it must have been on her, but she was very close too, or why did she live like a hermit when she could have had the friendship of the best?'

"'Perhaps because her brother overruled her; he has evidently had an eye on this property for a long time.'

"'Yes, but they have not even had the comforts. For three years at least no one has seen a butcher's cart stop at their door. How they have lived none of us know; yet there was no lack of money or their neighbors would have felt it their duty to look after them. Mrs. Wakeham has owned very valuable stocks, and as for her dividends, we know by what the postmaster says that they came regularly.'

"'This is very interesting,' said I. 'I thought that fellow's eyes showed a great deal of greed for the little he was likely to inherit. Is there no one who is fully acquainted with their affairs, or have they lived so long out of the pale of society that they possess no friends?'

"'I do not know of any one who has ever been honored with their confidence,' quoth the young lady. 'They have shown so plainly that they did not desire attention that gradually we have all ceased to go to their doors.'

"'And did not sickness make any difference? Did no one go near them when it was learned how ill this poor woman was?'

"'We did not know she was ill till this morning. We had missed her face at the window, but no doctor had been called, and no medicine bought, so we never thought her to be in any danger. When we did find it out we were afraid to invade premises which had been so long shut against us; at least I was; others did go, but they were received so coldly they did not remain; it is hard to stand up against the sullen displeasure of a man like Mr. Huckins.'

"'And do you mean to say that this man and his sister have lived there alone and unvisited for years?'

"'They wished it, Mr. Etheridge. They courted loneliness and rejected friendship. Only one person, Mr. H— —, the minister, has persisted in keeping up his old habit of calling once a year, but I have heard him say that he always dreaded the visit, first, because they made him see so plainly that they resented the intrusion, and, secondly, because each year showed him barer floors and greater evidences of poverty or determined avarice. What he will say now, when he hears about the two wills and the brother trying to run away with his sister's savings, before her body was cold, I do not know. There will be some indignation felt in town you may be sure, and considerable excitement. I hope you will come back to-morrow to help me answer questions.'

"'I shall come back as soon as I have been to Marston.'

"'So you are going to hunt up the heirs? I pray you may be successful.'

"'Do you know them? Have you ever heard anything about them?' I asked.

"'Oh, no. It must be forty years since Harriet Huckins ran away from home. To many it will be a revelation that such a person lives.'

"'And we do not even know that she does,' said I.

"'True, true, she may be dead, and then that hateful brother will have the whole. I hope he won't. I hope she is alive and will come here and make amends for the disgrace which that unsightly building has put upon the street.'

"'I hope so too,' said I, feeling my old disgust of Huckins renewed at this mention of him.

"We were now at her gate, so bidding her good-by, I turned away through the midnight streets, determined to find the constable. As I went hurrying along in the direction of his home, Miss Thompson's question repeated itself in my own mind. Had Mrs. Wakeham been the sufferer and victim which her appearance, yes and her words to me, had betokened? Or was her brother sincere in his passion and true in his complaints that he had been subject to her whims and had led the life of a dog in order to please her. With the remembrance of their two faces before me, I felt inclined to believe her words rather than his, and yet her last cry had contained something in its tone beside anxiety for the rights of an almost unknown heir; there had been anger in it,—the anger of one whose secret has been surprised and who feels himself personally robbed of something dearer than life.

"However, at this time I could not stop to weigh these possibilities or decide this question. Whatever was true as regarded the balance of right between these two, there was no doubt as to the fact that this man was not to be trusted under temptation. I therefore made what haste I could, and being fortunate enough to find the constable still up, succeeded in interesting him in the matter and obtaining his promise to have the house put under proper surveillance. This done, I took the car for Fulton Ferry, and was so fortunate as to reach home at or near two o'clock in the morning. This was last night, and to-day you see me here. You disappoint me by saying that you know no one by the name of Harriet Smith."

"Yet," exclaimed Edgar, rousing himself from his attitude of listening, "I know all the old inhabitants. Harriet Smith," he continued in a musing tone, "Harriet—What is there in the name that stirs up some faint recollection? Did I once know a person by that name after all?"

"Nothing more likely."

"But there the thing stops. I cannot get any farther," mused Edgar. "The name is not entirely new to me. I have some vague memory in connection with it, but what memory I cannot tell. Let me see if Jerry can help us." And going to the door, he called "Jerry! Jerry!"

The response came slowly; heavy bodies do not soon overcome their inertia. But after the lapse of a few minutes a shuffling footstep was heard. Then the sound of heavy breathing, something between a snore and a snort, and the huge form of the good-natured driver came slowly into view, till it paused and stood in the door opening, which it very nearly filled.

"Did you call, sirs?" asked he, with a rude attempt at a bow.

"Yes," responded Edgar, "I wanted to know if you remembered a woman by the name of Harriet Smith once living about here."

"Har-ri-et Smith," was the long-drawn-out reply; "Har-ri-et Smith! I knows lots of Harriets, and as for Smiths, they be as plenty as squirrels in nut time; but Har-ri-et Smith—I wouldn't like to say I didn't, and I wouldn't like to say I did."

"She is an old woman now, if she is still living," suggested Frank. "Or she may have moved away."

"Yes, sir, yes, of course"; and they perceived another slow Harriet begin to form itself upon his lips.

Seeing that he knew nothing of the person mentioned, Edgar motioned him away, but Frank, with a lawyer's belief in using all means at his command, stopped him as he was heavily turning his back and said:

"I have good news for a woman by that name. If you can find her, and she turns out to be a sister of Cynthia Wakeham, of Flatbush, New York, there will be something good for you too. Do you want to try for it?"

"Do I?" and the grin which appeared on Jerry's face seemed to light up the room. "I'm not quick," he hastily acknowledged, as if in fear that Frank would observe this fault and make use of it against him; "that is, I'm not spry on my feet, but that leaves me all the more time for gossip, and gossip is what'll do *this* business, isn't it, Dr. Sellick?" Edgar nodding, Jerry laughed, and Frank, seeing he had got an interested assistant at last, gave him such instructions as he thought he needed, and dismissed him to his work.

When he was gone, the friends looked for an instant at each other, and then Frank rose.

"I am going out," said he. "If you have friends to see or business to look after, don't think you must come with me. I always take a walk before retiring."

"Very well," replied Edgar, with unusual cheeriness. "Then if you will excuse me I'll not accompany you. Going to walk for pleasure? You'd better take the road north; the walk in that direction is the best in town."

"All right," returned Frank; "I'll not be gone more than an hour. See you again in the morning if not to-night." And with a careless nod he disappeared, leaving Edgar sitting alone in the room.

On the walk in front of the house he paused.

"To the north," he repeated, looking up and down the street, with a curious shake of the head; "good advice, no doubt, and one that I will follow some time, but not to-night. The attractions in an opposite direction are too great." And with an odd smile, which was at once full of manly confidence and dreamy anticipation, he turned his face southward and strode away through the warm and perfumed darkness of the summer night.

He took the road by which he had come from the depot, and passing rapidly by the few shops that clustered about the hotel, entered at once upon the street whose picturesque appearance had attracted his attention earlier in the evening.

What is he seeking? Exercise — the exhilaration of motion — the refreshment of change? If so, why does he look behind and before him with an almost guilty air as he advances towards a dimly lighted house, guarded by the dense branches of a double row of poplars? Is it here the attraction lies which has drawn him from the hotel and the companionship of his friend? Yes, for he stops as he reaches it and gazes first along the dim shadowy vista made by those clustered trunks and upright boughs, and then up the side and across the front of the silent house itself, while an expression of strange wistfulness softens the eager brightness of his face, and his smile becomes one of mingled pride and tenderness, for which the peaceful scene, with all its picturesque features, can scarcely account.

Can it be that his imagination has been roused and his affections stirred by the instantaneous vision of an almost unknown woman? that this swelling of the heart and this sudden turning of his whole nature towards what is sweetest, holiest, and most endearing in life means that his hitherto free spirit has met its mate, and that here in the lonely darkness, before a strange portal and in the midst of new and untried scenes, he has found the fate that comes once to every man, making him a changed being for ever after?

The month is June and the air is full of the scent of roses. He can see their fairy forms shining from amid the vines clambering over the walls and porches before him. They suggest all that is richest and spiciest and most exquisite in nature, as does her face as he remembered it. What if a thorn has rent a petal here and there, in the luxurious flowers before him, are they not roses still? So to him her face is all the lovelier for the blemish which might speak to others of imperfection, but which to him is only a call for profounder tenderness and more ardent devotion. And if in her nature there lies a fault also, is not a man's first love potent enough to overlook even that? He begins to think so, and allows his glances to roam from window to window of the nearly darkened house, as if half expecting her sweet and melancholy head to look forth in quest of the stars — or him.

The living rooms are mainly on the side that overlooks the garden, and scarcely understanding by what impulse he is swayed, he passes around the wall to a second gate, which he perceives opening at right angles to the poplar walk. Here he pauses a moment, looking up at the window which for some reason he has determined to be hers, and while he stands there, the moonlight shows the figure of another man coming from the highway and making towards the self-same spot. But before this second person reaches Frank he pauses, falters, and finally withdraws. Who is it? The shadow is on his face and we cannot see, but one thing is apparent, Frank Etheridge is not the only man who worships at this especial shrine to-night.

VI.
YOUNG MEN'S FANCIES.

The next morning at about nine o'clock Frank burst impetuously into Edgar's presence. They had not met for a good-night the evening before and they had taken breakfast separately.

"Edgar, what is this I hear about Hermione Cavanagh? Is it true she lives alone in that house with her sister, and that they neither of them ever go out, not even for a half-hour's stroll in the streets?"

Edgar, flushed at the other's excitement, turned and busied himself a moment with his books and papers before replying.

"Frank, you have been among the gossips."

"And what if I have! You would tell me nothing, and I knew there was a tragedy in her face; I saw it at the first glance."

"Is it a tragedy, this not going out?"

"It is the result of a tragedy; must be. They say nothing and nobody could draw from her beyond the boundary of that brick wall we rode by so carelessly. And she so young, so beautiful!"

"Frank, you exaggerate," was all the answer he received.

Frank bit his lip; the phrase he had used had been a trifle strong for the occasion. But in another moment he was ready to continue the conversation.

"Perhaps I do speak of an experiment that has never been tried; but you know what I mean. She has received some shock which has terrified her and made her afraid of the streets, and no one can subdue this fear or induce her to step through her own gate. Is not that sad and interesting enough to move a man who recognizes her beauty?"

"It is certainly very sad," quoth the other, "if it is quite true, which I doubt."

"Go talk to your neighbors then; they have not been absent like yourself for a good long year."

"I am not interested enough," the other began.

"But you ought to be," interpolated Frank. "As a physician you ought to recognize the peculiarities of such a prejudice. Why, if I had such a case— —"

"But the case is not mine. I am not and never have been Miss Cavanagh's physician."

"Well, well, her friend then."

"Who told you I was her friend?"

"I don't remember; I understood from some one that you used to visit her."

"My neighbors, as you call them, have good memories."

"*Did* you use to visit her?"

"Frank, Frank, subdue your curiosity. If I did, I do not now. The old gentleman is dead, and it was he upon whom I was accustomed to call when I went to their house."

"The old gentleman?"

"Miss Cavanagh's father."

"And you called upon him?"

"Sometimes."

"Edgar, how short you are."

"Frank, how impatient you are."

"But I have reason."

"How's that?"

"I want to hear about her, and you mock me with the most evasive replies."

Edgar turned towards his friend; the flush had departed from his features, but his manner certainly was not natural. Yet he did not look unkindly at the ardent young lawyer. On the contrary, there was a gleam of compassion in his eye, as he remarked, with more emphasis than he had before used:

"I am sorry if I seem to be evading any question you choose to put. But the truth is you seem to know more about the young lady than I do myself. I did not know that she was the victim of any such caprice."

"Yet it has lasted a year."

"A year?"

"Just the time you have been away."

"Just— —" Edgar paused in the repetition. Evidently his attention had been caught at last. But he soon recovered himself. "A strange coincidence," he laughed. "Happily it is nothing more."

Frank surveyed his friend very seriously.

"I shall believe you," said he.

"You may," was the candid rejoinder. And the young physician did not flinch, though Etheridge continued to look at him steadily and with undoubted intention. "And now what luck with Jerry?" he suddenly inquired, with a cheerful change of tone.

"None; I shall leave town at ten."

"Is there no Harriet Smith here?"

"Not if I can believe him."

"And has been none in the last twenty years?"

"Not that he can find out."

"Then your quest here is at an end?"

"No, it has taken another turn, that is all."

"You mean— —"

"That I shall come back here to-morrow. I must be sure that what Jerry says is true. Besides— — But why mince the matter? I—I have become interested in that girl, Edgar, and want to know her—hear her speak. Cannot you help me to make her acquaintance? If you used to go to the house— — Why do you frown? Do you not like Miss Cavanagh? "

Edgar hastily smoothed his forehead.

"Frank, I have never thought very much about her. She was young when I visited her father, and then that scar— —"

"Never mind," cried Frank. He felt as if a wound in his own breast had been touched.

Edgar was astonished. He was not accustomed to display his own feelings, and did not know what to make of a man who did. But he did not finish his sentence.

"If she does not go out," he observed instead, "she may be equally unwilling to receive visitors."

"Oh, no," the other eagerly broke in; "people visit there just the same. Only they say she never likes to hear anything about her peculiarity. She wishes it accepted without words."

It was now Edgar's turn to ask a question.

"You say she lives there alone? You mean with servants, doubtless?"

"Oh, yes, she has a servant. But I did not say she lived there alone; I said she and her sister."

Edgar was silent.

"Her sister does not go out, either, they say."

"No? What does it all mean?"

"That is what *I* want to know."

"Not go out? Emma!"

"Do you remember *Emma*?"

"Yes, she is younger than Hermione."

"And what kind of a girl is *she*?"

"Don't ask me, Frank. I have no talent for describing beautiful women."

"She is beautiful, then?"

"If her sister is, yes."

"You mean *she* has no scar." It was softly said, almost reverently.

"No, she has no scar."

Frank shook his head.

"The scar appeals to me, Edgar."

Edgar smiled, but it was not naturally. The constraint in his manner had increased rather than diminished, and he seemed anxious to start upon the round of calls he had purposed to make.

"You must excuse me," said he, "I shall have to be off. You are coming back to-morrow?"

"If business does not detain me."

"You will find me in my new office by that time. I have rented the small brown house you must have noticed on the main street. Come there, and if you do not mind bachelor housekeeping, stay with me while you remain in town. I shall have a good cook, you may be sure, and as for a room, the north chamber has already been set apart for you."

Frank's face softened and he grasped the doctor's hand.

"That's good of you; it looks as if you expected me to need it."

"Have you not a Harriet Smith to find?"

Frank shrugged his shoulders. "I see that you understand lawyers."

Frank rode down to the depot with Jerry. As he passed Miss Cavanagh's house he was startled to perceive a youthful figure bending over the flower-beds on the inner side of the wall. "She is not so pretty by daylight," was his first thought. But at that moment she raised her head, and with a warm thrill he recognized the fact that it was not Hermione, but the sister he was looking at.

It gave him something to think of, for this sister was not without her attractions, though they were less brilliant and also less marred than those of the sad and stately Hermione.

When he arrived at his office his first inquiry was if anything had been heard from Flatbush, and upon being told to the contrary he immediately started for that place. He found the house a scene of some tumult. Notwithstanding the fact that the poor woman still lay unburied, the parlors and lower hall were filled with people, who stared at the walls and rapped with wary but eager knuckles on the various lintels and casements. Whispers of a treasure having been found beneath the boards of the flooring had reached the ear of the public, and the greatest curiosity had been raised in the breasts of those who up to this day had looked upon the house as a worm-eaten structure fit only for the shelter of dogs.

Mr. Dickey was in a room above, and to him Frank immediately hastened.

"Well," said he, "what news?"

"Ah," cried the jovial witness, coming forward, "glad to see you. Have you found the heirs?"

"Not yet," rejoined Frank. "Have you had any trouble? I thought I saw a police-officer below."

"Yes, we had to have some one with authority here. Even Huckins agreed to that; he is afraid the house will be run away with, I think. Did you see what a crowd has assembled in the parlors? We let them in so that Huckins won't seem to be the sole object of suspicion; but he really is, you know. He gave me plenty to do that night."

"He did, did he?"

"Yes; you had scarcely gone before he began his tactics. First he led me very politely to a room where there was a bed; then he brought me a bottle of the vilest rum you ever drank; and then he sat down to be affable. While he talked I was at ease, but when he finally got up and said he would try to get a snatch of sleep I grew suspicious, and stopped drinking the rum and set myself to listening. He went directly to a room not far from me and shut himself in. He had no light, but in a few minutes I heard him strike a match, and then another and another. 'He is searching under the boards for more treasure,' thought I, and creeping into the next room I was fortunate enough to come upon a closet so old and with such big cracks in its partition that I was enabled to look through them into the place where he was. The sight that met my eye was startling. He was, as I conjectured, peering under the boards, which he had ripped up early in the evening; and as he had only the light of a match to aid him, I would catch quick glimpses of his eager, peering face and then lose the sight of it in sudden darkness till the gleam of another match came to show it up again. He crouched upon the floor and crept along the whole length of the board, thrusting in his arm to right and left, while the sweat oozed on his forehead and fell in large drops into the long, narrow hollow beneath him. At last he seemed to grow wild with repeated disappointments, and, starting up, stood looking about him at the four surrounding walls, as if demanding them to give up their secrets. Then the match went out, and I heard him stamp his foot with rage before proceeding to put back the boards and shift them into place. Then there came silence, during which I crept on tiptoe to the place I had left, judging that he would soon leave his room and return to see if I had been watching him.

"The box was on the bed, and throwing myself beside it, I grasped it with one arm and hid my face with the other, and as I lay there I soon became conscious of his presence, and I knew he was looking from me to the box, and weighing the question as to whether I was sleeping sound enough for him to risk a blow. But I did not stir, though I almost expected a sudden crash on my head, and in another moment he crept away, awed possibly by my superior strength, for I am a much bigger man than he, as you must see. When I thought him gone I dropped my arm and looked up. The room was in total darkness. Bounding to my feet I followed him through the halls and came upon him in the room of death. He had the lamp in his hand, and he was standing over his sister with an awful look on his face.

"'Where have you hidden it?' he hissed to the senseless form before him. 'That box is not all you had. Where are the bonds and the stocks, and the money I helped you to save?'

"He was so absorbed he did not see me. He stooped by the bed and ran his hand along under the mattresses; then he lifted the pillows and looked under the bed. Then he rose and trod gingerly over the floor, as if to see if any of the boards were loose, and peered into the empty closet, and felt with wary hand up and down the mantel sides. At last his eyes fell on the clock, and he was about to lift his hand to it when I said:

"'The clock is all right; you needn't set it; see, it just agrees with my watch!'

"What a face he turned to me! I tell you it is no fun to meet such eyes in an empty house at one o'clock at night; and if you hadn't told me the police would be within call I should have been sick enough of my job, I can tell you. As it was, I drew back a foot or two and hugged the box a little more tightly, while he, with a coward's bravado, stepped after me and whispered below his breath:

"'You are making yourself too much at home here. If I want to stop the clock, now that my sister is dead, what is that to you? You have no respect for a house in mourning, and I am free to tell you so.'

"To this tirade I naturally made no answer, and he turned again to the clock. But just as I was asking myself whether I should stop him or let him go on with his peerings and pokings, the bell rang loudly below. It was a welcome interruption to me, but it made him very angry. However, he went down and welcomed, as decently as he knew how, a woman who had been sent to his assistance by Miss Thompson, evidently thinking that it was time he made some effort to regain my good opinion by avoiding all further cause for suspicion.

"At all events, he gave me no more trouble that night, nor since, though the way he haunts the door of that room and the looks he casts inside at the clock are enough to make one's blood run cold. Do you think there are any papers hidden there?"

"I have no doubt of it," returned Frank. "Do you remember that the old woman's last words were, 'The clock! the clock!' As soon as I can appeal to the Surrogate I shall have that piece of furniture examined."

"I shall be mortally interested in knowing what you find there," commented Mr. Dickey. "If the property comes to much, won't Miss Thompson and I get something out of it for our trouble?"

"No doubt," said Frank.

"Then we will get married," said he, and looked so beaming, that Frank shook him cordially by the hand.

"But where is Huckins?" the lawyer now inquired. "I didn't see him down below."

"He is chewing his nails in the kitchen. He is like a dog with a bone; you cannot get him to leave the house for a moment."

"I must see him," said Frank, and went down the back stairs to the place where he had held his previous interview with this angry and disappointed man.

At first sight of the young lawyer Huckins flushed deeply, but he soon grew pale and obsequious, as if he had held bitter communing with himself through the last thirty-six hours, and had resolved to restrain his temper for the future in the presence of the man who understood him. But he could not help a covert sneer from creeping into his voice.

"Have you found the heirs?" he asked, bowing with ill-mannered grace, and pushing forward the only chair there was in the room.

"I shall find them when I need them," rejoined Frank. "Fortunes, however small, do not usually go begging."

"Then you have not found them?" the other declared, a hard glitter of triumph shining in his sinister eye.

"I have not brought them with me," acknowledged the lawyer, warily.

"Perhaps, then, you won't," suggested Huckins, while he seemed to grow instantly at least two inches in stature. "If they are not in Marston where are they? Dead! And that leaves me the undisputed heir to all my sister's savings."

"I do not believe them dead," protested Frank.

"Why?" Huckins half smiled, half snarled.

"Some token of the fact would have come to you. You are not in a strange land or in unknown parts; you are living in the old homestead where this lost sister of yours was reared. You would have heard if she had died, at least so it strikes an unprejudiced mind."

"Then let it strike yours to the contrary," snapped out his angry companion. "When she went away it was in anger and with the curse of her father ringing in her ears. Do you see that porch?" And Huckins pointed through the cracked windows to a decayed pair of steps leading from the side of the house. "It was there she ran down on her way out. I see her now, though forty years have passed, and I, a little fellow of six, neither understood nor appreciated what was happening. My father stood in the window above, and he cried out: 'Don't come back! You have chosen your way, now go in it. Let me never see you nor hear from you again.' And we never did, never! And now you tell me we would have heard if she had died. You don't know the heart of folks if you say that. Harriet cut herself adrift that day, and she knew it."

"Yet you were acquainted with the fact that she went to Marston."

The indignant light in the brother's eye settled into a look of cunning.

"Oh," he acknowledged carelessly, "we heard so at the time, when everything was fresh. But we heard nothing more, nothing."

"Nothing?" Frank repeated. "Not that she had married and had had children?"

"No," was the dogged reply. "My sister up there," and Huckins jerked his hand towards the room where poor Mrs. Wakeham lay, "surmised things, but she didn't know anything for certain. If she had she might have sent for these folks long ago. She had time enough in the last ten years we have been living in this hole together."

"But," Etheridge now ventured, determined not to be outmatched in cunning, "you say she was penurious, too penurious to live comfortably or to let you do so."

Huckins shrugged his shoulders and for a moment looked balked; then he cried: "The closest women have their whims. If she had known any such folks to have been living as you have named, she would have sent for them."

"If you had let her," suggested Frank.

Huckins turned upon him and his eye flashed. But he very soon cringed again and attempted a sickly smile, which completed the disgust the young lawyer felt for him.

"If I had let her," he repeated; "I, who pined for companionship or anything which would have put a good meal into my mouth! You do not know me, sir; you are prejudiced against me because I want my earnings, and a little comfort in my old age."

"If I am prejudiced against you, it is yourself who has made me so," returned the other. "Your conduct has not been of a nature to win my regard, since I have had the honor of your acquaintance."

"And what has yours been, worming, as you have, into my sister's confidence——"

But here Frank hushed him. "We will drop this," said he. "You know me, and I think I know you. I came to give you one last chance to play the man by helping me to find your relatives. I see you have no intention of doing so, so I will now proceed to find them without you."

"If they exist," he put in.

"Certainly, if they exist. If they do not——"

"What then?"

"I must have proofs to that effect. I must know that your sister left no heirs but yourself."

"That will take time," he grumbled. "I shall be kept weeks out of my rights."

"The Surrogate will see that you do not suffer."

He shuddered and looked like a fox driven into his hole.

"It is shameful, shameful!" he cried. "It is nothing but a conspiracy to rob me of my own. I suppose I shall not be allowed to live in my own house." And his eyes wandered greedily over the rafters above him.

"Are you sure that it is yours?"

"Yes, yes, damn you!" But the word had been hasty, and he immediately caught Frank's sleeve and cringed in contrition. "I beg your pardon," he cried, "perhaps we had better not talk any longer, for I have been too tried for patience. They will not even leave me alone in my grief," he whined, pointing towards the rooms full, as I have said, of jostling neighbors and gossips.

"It will be quiet enough after the funeral," Frank assured him.

"Oh! oh! the funeral!" he groaned.

"Is it going to be too extravagant?" Frank insinuated artfully.

Huckins gave the lawyer a look, dropped his eyes and mournfully shook his head.

"The poor woman would not have liked it," he muttered; "but one must be decent towards one's own blood."

VII.
THE WAY OPENS.

Frank succeeded in having Mr. Dickey appointed as Custodian of the property, then he went back to Marston.

"Good-evening, Doctor; what a nest of roses you have here for a bachelor," was his jovial cry, as he entered the quaint little house, in which Sellick had now established himself. "I declare, when you told me I should always find a room here, I did not realize what a temptation you were offering me. And in sight——" He paused, changing color as he drew back from the window to which he had stepped,——"of the hills," he somewhat awkwardly added.

Edgar, who had watched the movements of his friend from under half lowered lids, smiled dryly.

"*Of the hills,*" he repeated. Then with a short laugh, added, "I knew that you liked that especial view."

Frank's eye, which was still on a certain distant chimney, lighted up wonderfully as he turned genially towards his friend.

"I did not know you were such a good fellow," he laughed. "I hope you have found yourself made welcome here."

"Oh, yes, welcome enough."

"Any patients yet?"

"All of Dudgeon's, I fear. I have been doing little else but warning one man after another: 'Now, no words against any former practitioner. If you want help from me, tell me your symptoms, but don't talk about any other doctor's mistakes, for I have not time to hear it.'"

"Poor old Dudgeon!" cried Frank. Then, shortly: "I'm a poor one to hide my impatience. Have you seen either of *them* yet?"

"Either—of—them?"

"The girls, the two sweet whimsical girls. You know whom I mean, Edgar."

"You only spoke of one when you were here before, Frank."

"And I only think of one. But I saw the other on my way to the depot, and that made me speak of the two. Have you seen them?"

"No," answered the other, with unnecessary dryness; "I think you told me they did not go out."

"But you have feet, man, and you can go to them, and I trusted that you would, if only to prepare the way for me; for I mean to visit them, as you have every reason to believe, and I should have liked an introducer."

"Frank," asked the other, quietly, but with a certain marked earnestness, "has it gone as deep as that? Are you really serious in your intention of making the acquaintance of Miss Cavanagh?"

"Serious? Have you for a minute thought me otherwise?"

"You are not serious in most things."

"In business I am, and in— —"

"Love?" the other smiled.

"Yes, if you can call it love, yet."

"We will not call it anything," said the other. "You want to see her, that is all. I wonder at your decision, but can say nothing against it. Happily, you have seen her defect."

"It is not a defect to me."

"Not if it is in her nature as well?"

"Her nature?"

"A woman who for any reason cuts herself off from her species, as she is said to do, cannot be without her faults. Such idiosyncrasies do not grow out of the charity we are bid to have for our fellow-creatures."

"But she may have suffered. I can readily believe she has suffered from that same want of charity in others. There is nothing like a personal defect to make one sensitive. Think of the averted looks she must have met from many thoughtless persons; and she almost a beauty!"

"Yes, that *almost* is tragic."

"It can excuse much."

Edgar shook his head. "Think what you are doing, Frank, that's all. I should hesitate in making the acquaintance of one who for *any* reason has shut herself away from the world."

"Is not her whim shared by her sister?"

"They say so."

"Then there are two whose acquaintance you would hesitate to make?"

"Certainly, if I had any ulterior purpose beyond that of mere acquaintanceship."

"Her sister has no scar?"

Edgar, weary, perhaps, of the conversation, did not answer.

"Why should she shut herself up?" mused Frank, too interested in the subject to note the other's silence.

"Women are mysteries," quoth Edgar, shortly.

"But this is more than a mystery," cried Frank. "Whim will not account for it. There must be something in the history of these two girls which the world does not know."

"That is not the fault of the world," retorted Edgar, in his usual vein of sarcasm.

But Frank was reckless. "The world is right to be interested," he avowed. "It would take a very cold heart not to be moved with curiosity by such a fact as two girls secluding themselves in their own house, without any manifest reason. Are *you* not moved by it, Edgar? Are you, indeed, as indifferent as you seem?"

"I should like to know why they do this, of course, but I shall not busy myself to find out. I have much else to do."

"Well, I have not. It is the one thing in life for me; so look out for some great piece of audacity on my part, for speak to her I will, and that, too, before I leave the town."

"I do not see how you will manage that, Frank."

"You forget I am a lawyer."

Yet for all the assurance manifested by this speech, it was some time before Frank could see his way clearly to what he desired. A dozen plans were made and dismissed as futile before he finally determined to seek the assistance of a fellow-lawyer whose name he had seen in the window of the one brick building in the principal street. "Through him," thought he, "I may light upon some business which will enable me to request with propriety an interview with Miss Cavanagh." Yet his heart failed him as he went up the steps of Mr. Hamilton's office, and if that gentleman, upon presenting himself, had been a young man, Frank would certainly have made some excuse for his intrusion, and retired. But he was old and white-haired and benignant, and so Frank was lured into introducing himself as a young lawyer from New York, engaged in finding the whereabouts of one Harriet Smith, a former resident of Marston.

Mr. Hamilton, who could not fail to be impressed by Etheridge's sterling appearance, met him with cordiality.

"I have heard of you," said he, "but I fear your errand here is bound to be fruitless. No Harriet Smith, so far as I know, ever came to reside in this town. And I was born and bred in this street. Have you actual knowledge that one by that name ever lived here, and can you give me the date?"

The answers Frank made were profuse but hurried; he had not expected to gain news of Harriet Smith; he had only used the topic as a means of introducing conversation. But when he came to the point in which he was more nearly interested, he found his courage fail him. He could not speak the name of Miss Cavanagh, even in the most casual fashion, and so the interview ended without any further result than the making on his part of a pleasant acquaintance. Subdued by his failure, Frank quitted the office, and walked slowly down the street. If he had not boasted of his intentions to Edgar, he would have left the town without further effort; but now his pride was involved, and he made that an excuse to his love. Should he proceed boldly to her house, use the knocker, and ask to see Miss Cavanagh? Yes, he might do that, but afterwards? With what words should he greet her, or win that confidence which the situation so peculiarly demanded? He was not an acknowledged friend, or the friend of an acknowledged friend, unless Edgar— — But no, Edgar was not their friend; it would be folly to speak his name to them. What then? Must he give up his hopes till time had paved the way to their realization? He feared it must be so, yet he recoiled from the delay. In this mood he re-entered Edgar's office.

A woman in hat and cloak met him.

"Are you the stranger lawyer that has come to town?" she asked.

He bowed, wondering if he was about to hear news of Harriet Smith.

"Then this note is for you," she declared, handing him a little three-cornered billet.

His heart gave a great leap, and he turned towards the window as he opened the note. Who could be writing letters to him of such dainty appearance as this? Not she, of course, and yet— — He tore open the sheet, and read these words:

> "If not asking too great a favor, may I request that you will call
> at my house, in your capacity of lawyer.

"As I do not leave my own home, you will pardon this informal method of requesting your services. The lawyer here cannot do my work.

"Yours respectfully,

"Hermione Cavanagh."

He was too much struck with amazement and delight to answer the messenger at once. When he did so, his voice was very business-like.

"Will Miss Cavanagh be at liberty this morning?" he asked. "I shall be obliged to return to the city after dinner."

"She told me to say that any time would be convenient to her," was the answer.

"Then say to her that I will be at her door in half an hour."

The woman nodded, and turned.

"She lives on the road to the depot, where the two rows of poplars are," she suddenly declared, as she paused at the door.

"I know," he began, and blushed, for the woman had given him a quick glance of surprise. "I noticed the poplars," he explained.

She smiled as she passed out, and that made him crimson still more.

"Do I wear my heart on my sleeve?" he murmured to himself, in secret vexation. "If so, I must wrap it about with a decent cloak of reserve before I go into the presence of one who has such power to move it." And he was glad Edgar was not at home to mark his excitement.

The half hour wore away, and he stood on the rose-embowered porch. Would she come to the door herself, or would it be the sad-eyed sister he should see first? It mattered little. It was Hermione who had sent for him, and it was with Hermione he should talk. Was it his heart that was beating so loudly? He had scarcely answered the question, when the door opened, and the woman who had served as a messenger from Miss Cavanagh stood before him.

"Ah!" said she, "come in." And in another moment he was in the enchanted house.

A door stood open at his left, and into the room thus disclosed he was ceremoniously ushered.

"Miss Cavanagh will be down in a moment," said the woman, as she slowly walked away, with more than one lingering backward look.

He did not note this look, for his eyes were on the quaint old furniture and shadowy recesses of the staid best room, in which he stood an uneasy guest. For somehow he had imagined he would see the woman of his dreams in a place of cheer and sunshine; at a window, perhaps, where the roses looked in, or at least in a spot enlivened by some evidences of womanly handiwork and taste. But here all was stiff as at a funeral. The high black mantel-shelf was without clock or vase, and the only attempt at ornament to be seen within the four grim walls was an uncouth wreath, made of shells, on a background of dismal black, which hung between the windows. It was enough to rob any moment of its romance. And yet, if she should look fair here, what might he not expect of her beauty in more harmonious surroundings.

As he was adjusting his ideas to this thought, there came the sound of a step on the stair, and the next moment Hermione Cavanagh entered his presence.

VIII.
A SEARCH AND ITS RESULTS.

Hermione Cavanagh, without the scar, would have been one of the handsomest of women. She was of the grand type, with height and a nobility of presence to which the extreme loveliness of her perfect features lent a harmonizing grace. Of a dazzling complexion, the hair which lay above her straight fine brows shone ebon-like in its lustre, while her eyes, strangely and softly blue, filled the gazer at first with surprise and then with delight as the varying emotions of her quick mind deepened them into a more perfect consonance with her hair, or softened them into something like the dewy freshness of heaven-born flowers. Her mouth was mobile, but the passions it expressed were not of the gentlest, whatever might be the language of her eyes, and so it was that her face was in a way a contradiction of itself, which made it a fascinating study to one who cared to watch it, or possessed sufficient understanding to read its subtle language. She was oddly dressed in a black, straight garment, eminently in keeping with the room; but there was taste displayed in the arrangement of her hair, and nothing could make her face anything but a revelation of beauty, unless it was the scar, and that Frank Etheridge did not see.

"Are you—" she began and paused, looking at him with such surprise that he felt his cheeks flush—"the lawyer who was in town a few days ago on some pressing inquiry?"

"I am," returned Frank, making her the low bow her embarrassment seemed to demand.

"Then you must excuse me," said she; "I thought you were an elderly man, like our own Mr. Hamilton. I should not have sent for you if——"

"If you had known I had no more experience," he suggested, with a smile, seeing her pause in some embarrassment.

She bowed; yet he knew that was not the way she would have ended the sentence if she had spoken her thought.

"Then I am to understand," said he, with a gentleness born of his great wish to be of service to her, "that you would prefer that I should send you an older adviser. I can do it, Miss Cavanagh."

"Thank you," she said, and stood hesitating, the slight flush on her cheek showing that she was engaged in some secret struggle. "I will tell you my difficulty," she pursued at last, raising her eyes with a frank look to his face. "Will you be seated?"

Charmed with the graciousness of her manner when once relieved from embarrassment, he waited for her to sit and then took a chair himself.

"It is a wearisome affair," she declared, "but one which a New York lawyer can solve without much trouble." And with the clearness of a highly cultivated mind, she gave him the facts of a case in which she and her sister had become involved through the negligence of her man of business.

"Can you help me?" she asked.

"Very easily," he replied. "You have but to go to New York and swear to these facts before a magistrate, and the matter will be settled without difficulty."

"But I cannot go to New York."

"No? Not on a matter of this importance?"

"On no matter. I do not travel, Mr. Etheridge."

The pride and finality with which this was uttered, gave him his first glimpse of the hard streak which there was undoubtedly in her character. Though he longed to press the question he judged that he had better not, so suggested carelessly:

"Your sister, then?"

But she met this suggestion, as he had expected her to, with equal calmness and pride.

"My sister does not travel either."

He looked the astonishment he did not feel and remarked gravely:

"I fear, then, that the matter cannot be so easily adjusted." And he began to point out the difficulties in the way, to all of which she listened with a slightly absent air, as if the affair was in reality of no great importance to her.

Suddenly she waved her hand with a quick gesture.

"You can do as you please," said she. "If you can save us from loss, do so; if not, let the matter go; I shall not allow it to worry me further." Then she looked up at him with a total change of expression, and for the first time the hint of a smile softened the almost severe outline of her mouth. "You are searching, I hear, for a woman named Harriet Smith; have you found her, sir?"

Delighted at this evidence on her part of a wish to indulge in general conversation, he answered with alacrity:

"Not yet. She was not, as it seems, a well-known inhabitant of this town as I had been led to believe. I even begin to fear she never has lived here at all. The name is a new one to you, I presume."

"Smith. Can the name of Smith ever be said to be new?" she laughed with something like an appearance of gayety.

"But Harriet," he explained, "Harriet Smith, once Harriet Huckins."

"I never knew any Harriet Smith," she averred. "Would it have obliged you very much if I had?"

He smiled, somewhat baffled by her manner, but charmed by her voice, which was very rich and sweet in its tones.

"It certainly would have saved me much labor and suspense," he replied.

"Then the matter is serious?"

"Is not all law-business serious?"

"You have just proved it so," she remarked.

He could not understand her; she seemed to wish to talk and yet hesitated with the words on her lips. After waiting for her to speak further and waiting in vain, he changed the subject back to the one which had at first occupied them.

"I shall be in Marston again," said he; "if you will allow me I will then call again and tell you exactly what I can do for your interest."

"If you will be so kind," she replied, and seemed to breathe easier.

"I have one intimate friend in town," pursued Frank, as he rose to take his departure, "Dr. Sellick. If you know him— —"

Why did he pause? She had not moved and yet something, he could not say what, had made an entire change in her attitude and expression. It was as if a chill had passed over her, stiffening her limbs and paling her face, yet her eyes did not fall from his face, and she tried to speak as usual.

"Dr. Sellick?"

"Yes, he has returned to Marston after a year of absence. Have not the gossips told you that?"

"No; that is, I have seen no one—I used to know Dr. Sellick," she added with a vain attempt to be natural. "Is that my sister I hear?" And she turned sharply about.

Up to this moment she had uniformly kept the uninjured side of her face towards him, and he had noticed the fact and been profoundly touched by her seeming sensitiveness. But he was more touched now by the emotion which made her forget herself, for it argued badly for his hopes, and assured him that for all Sellick's assumed indifference, there had been some link of feeling between these two which he found himself illy prepared to accept.

"May I not have the honor," he requested, "of an introduction to your sister?"

"She is not coming; I was mistaken," was her sole reply, and her beautiful face turned once more towards him, with a deepening of its usual tragic expression which lent to it a severity which would have appalled most men. But he loved every change in that enigmatical countenance, there was so much character in its grave lines. So with the consideration that was a part of his nature he made a great effort to subdue his jealous curiosity, and saying, "Then we will reserve that pleasure till another time," bowed like a man at his ease, and passed quickly out of the door.

Yet his heart was heavy and his thoughts in wildest turmoil; for he loved this woman and she had paled and showed the intensest emotion at the mention of a man whom he had heard decry her. He might have felt worse could he have seen the look of misery which settled upon her face as the door closed upon him, or noted how long she sat with fixed eyes and paling lips in that dreary old parlor where he had left her. As it was, he felt sufficiently disturbed and for a long time hesitated whether or not he should confront Edgar with an accusation of knowing Miss Cavanagh better than he acknowledged. But Sellick's reserve was one that imposed silence, and Frank dared not break through it lest he should lose the one opportunity he now had of visiting Marston freely. So he composed himself with the thought that he had at least gained a footing in the house, and if the rest did not follow he had only himself to blame. And in this spirit he again left Marston.

He found plenty of work awaiting him in his office. Foremost in interest was an invitation to be present at the search which was to be instituted that afternoon in the premises of the Widow Wakeham. The will of which he had been made Executor, having been admitted to probate, it had been considered advisable to have an an inventory made of the personal effects of the deceased, and this day had been set apart for the purpose. To meet this appointment he hurried all the rest, and at the hour set, he found himself before the broken gate and gardens of the ruinous old house in Flatbush. There was a crowd already gathered there, and as he made his appearance he was greeted by a loud murmur which amply proved that his errand was known. At the door he was met by the two Appraisers appointed by the Surrogate, and within he found one or two workmen hobnobbing with a detective from police headquarters.

The house looked barer and more desolate than ever. It was a sunshiny day, and the windows having been opened, the pitiless rays streamed in showing all the defects which time and misuse had created in the once stately mansion. Not a crack in plastering or woodwork but stood forth in bold relief that day, nor were the gaping holes in the flooring of hall and parlor able to hide themselves any longer under the strips of carpet with which Huckins had endeavored to conceal them.

"Shall we begin with the lower floor?" asked one of the workmen, poising the axe he had brought with him.

The Appraisers bowed, and the work of demolition began. As the first sound of splitting boards rang through the empty house, a quick cry as of a creature in pain burst from the staircase without, and they saw, crouching there with trembling hands held out in protest, the meagre form of Huckins.

"Oh, don't! don't!" he began; but before they could answer, he had bounded down the stairs to where they stood and was looking with eager, staring eyes into the hole which the workmen had made.

"Have you found anything?" he asked. "It is to be all mine, you know, and the more you find the richer I'll be. Let's see—let's see, she may have hidden something here, there is no knowing." And falling on his knees he thrust his long arm into the aperture before him, just as Mr. Dickey had seen him do in a similar case on the night of the old woman's death.

But as his interference was not desired, he was drawn quietly back, and was simply allowed to stand there and watch while the others proceeded in their work. This he did with an excitement which showed itself in alternate starts and sudden breathless gasps, which, taken with the sickly smiles with which he endeavored to hide the frowns caused by his natural indignation, made a great impression upon Frank, who had come to regard him as a unique specimen in nature, something between a hyena and a fox.

As the men held up a little packet which had at last come to light very near the fireplace, he gave a shriek and stretched out two clutching hands.

"Let me have it!" he cried. "I know what that is; it disappeared from my sister's desk five years ago, and I could never get her to tell where she had put it. Let me have it, and I will open it here before you all. Indeed I will, sirs— though it is all mine, as I have said before."

But Etheridge, quietly taking it, placed it in his pocket, and Huckins sank back with a groan.

The next place to be examined was the room upstairs. Here the poor woman had spent most of her time till she was seized with her last sickness, and here the box had been found by Huckins, and here they expected to find the rest of her treasures. But beyond a small casket of almost worthless jewelry, nothing new was discovered, and they proceeded at Frank's suggestion to inspect the room where she had died, and where the clock still stood towards which she had lifted her dying hand, while saying, "There! there!"

As they approached this place, Huckins was seen to tremble. Catching Frank by the arm, he whispered:

"Can they be trusted? Are they honest men? She had greenbacks, piles of greenbacks; I have caught her counting them. If they find them, will they save them all for me?"

"They will save them all for the heir," retorted Frank, severely. "Why do you say they are for you, when you know you will only get them in default of other heirs being found."

"Why? why? Because I feel that they are mine. Heirs or no heirs, they will come into my grasp yet, and you of the law cannot help it. Do I look like a man who will die poor? No, no; but I don't want to be cheated. I don't want these men to rob me of anything which will rightfully be mine some day."

"You need not fret about that," said Frank. "No one will rob *you*," and he drew disdainfully aside.

The Appraisers had now surveyed the room awful with hideous memories to the young lawyer. Pointing to the bed, they said:

"Search that," and the search was made.

A bundle of letters came to light and were handed over to Frank.

"Why did she hide those away?" screamed Huckins. "They ain't money."

Nobody answered him.

The lintels of the windows and doors were now looked into, and the fireplace dismantled and searched. But nothing was found in these places, nor in the staring cupboards or beneath the loosened boards. Finally they came to the clock.

"Oh, let me," cried Huckins, "let me be the first to stop that clock. It has been running ever since I was a little boy. My mother used to wind it with her own hands. I cannot bear a stranger's hand to touch it. My—my sister would not have liked it."

But they disregarded even this appeal; and he was forced to stand in the background and see the old piece taken down and laid at length upon the floor with its face to the boards. There was nothing in its interior but the works which belonged there, but the frame at its back seemed unusually heavy, and Etheridge consequently had this taken off, when, to the astonishment of all and to the frantic delight of Huckins, there appeared at the very first view, snugly laid between the true and false backing, layers of bills and piles of sealed and unsealed papers.

"A fortune! A fortune!" cried this would-be possessor of his sister's hoarded savings. "I knew we should find it at last. I knew it wasn't all in that box. She tried to make me think it was, and made a great secret of where she had put it, and how it was all to be for me if I only let it alone. But the fortune was here in this old clock I have stared at a thousand times. Here, here, and I never knew it, never suspected it till — — "

He felt the lawyer's eyes fall on him, and became suddenly silent.

"Let's count it!" he greedily cried, at last.

But the Appraisers, maintaining their composure, motioned the almost frenzied man aside, and summoning Frank to assist them, made out a list of the papers, which were most of them valuable, and then proceeded to count the loose bills. The result was to make Huckins' eyes gleam with joy and satisfaction. As the last number left their lips, he threw up his arms in unrestrained glee, and cried:

"I will make you all rich some day. Yes, sirs; I have not the greed of my poor dead sister; I intend to spend what is mine, and have a good time while I live. I don't intend any one to dance over my grave when I am dead."

His attitude was one so suggestive of this very same expression of delight, that more than one who saw him and heard these words shuddered as they turned from him; but he did not care for cold shoulders now, or for any expression of disdain or disapproval. He had seen the fortune of his sister with his own eyes, and for that moment it was enough.

IX.
THE TWO SISTERS.

When Frank returned again to Marston he did not hesitate to tell Edgar that "he had business relations with Miss Cavanagh." This astonished the doctor, who was of a more conservative nature, but he did not mingle his astonishment with any appearance of chagrin, so Frank took heart, and began to dream that he had been mistaken in the tokens which Miss Cavanagh had given of being moved by the news of Dr. Sellick's return.

He went to see her as soon as he had supped with his friend, and this time he was introduced into a less formal apartment. Both sisters were present, and in the moment which followed the younger's introduction, he had leisure to note the similarity and dissimilarity between them, which made them such a delightful study to an interested observer.

Emma was the name of the younger, and as she had the more ordinary and less poetic name, so at first view she had the more ordinary and less poetic nature. Yet as the eye lingered on her touching face, with its unmistakable lines of sadness, the slow assurance gained upon the mind that beneath her quiet smile and gentle self-contained air lay the same force of will which spoke at once in the firm lip and steady gaze of the older woman. But her will was beneficent, and her character noble, while Hermione bore the evidences of being under a cloud, whose shadow was darkened by something less easily understood than sorrow.

Yet Hermione, and not Emma, moved his heart, and if he acknowledged to himself that a two-edged sword lay beneath the forced composure of her manner, it was with the same feelings with which he acknowledged the scar which offended all eyes but his own. They were both dressed in white, and Emma wore a cluster of snowy pinks in her belt, but Hermione was without ornament. The beauty of the latter was but faintly shadowed in her younger sister's face, yet had Emma been alone she would have stood in his mind as a sweet picture of melancholy young womanhood.

Hermione was evidently glad to see him. Fresh and dainty as this, their living room, looked, with its delicate white curtains blowing in the twilight breeze, there were hours, no doubt, when it seemed no more than a prison-house to these two passionate young hearts. To-night cheer and an emanation from the large outside world had come into it with their young visitor, and both girls seemed sensible of it, and brightened visibly. The talk was, of course, upon business, and while he noticed that Hermione led the conversation, he also noticed that when Emma did speak it was with the same clear grasp of the subject which he had admired in the other. "Two keen minds," thought he, and became more deeply interested than ever in the mystery of their retirement, and evident renouncement of the world.

He had to tell them he could do nothing for them unless one or both of them would consent to go to New York.

"The magistrate whom I saw," said he, "asked if you were well, and when I was forced to say yes, answered that for no other reason than illness could he excuse you from appearing before him. So if you will not comply with his rules, I fear your cause must go, and with it whatever it involves."

Emma, whose face showed the greater anxiety of the two, started as he said this, and glanced eagerly at her sister. But Hermione did not answer that glance. She was, perhaps, too much engaged in maintaining her own self-control, for the lines deepened in her face, and she all at once assumed that air of wild yet subdued suffering which had made him feel at the time of his first stolen glimpse of her face that it was the most tragic countenance he had ever beheld.

"We cannot go," came forth sharply from her lips, after a short but painful pause. "The case must be dropped." And she rose, as if she could not bear the weight of her thoughts, and moved slowly to the window, where she leaned for a moment, her face turned blankly on the street without.

Emma sighed, and her eyes fell with a strange pathos upon Frank's almost equally troubled face.

"There is no use," her gentle looks seemed to say. "Do not urge her; it will be only one grief the more."

But Frank was not one to heed such an appeal in sight of the noble drooping figure and set white face of the woman upon whose happiness he had fixed his own, though neither of these two knew it as yet. So, with a deprecating look at Emma, he crossed to Hermione's side, and with a slow, respectful voice exclaimed:

"Do not make me feel as if I had been the cause of loss to you. An older man might have done better. Let me send an older man to you, then, or pray that you reconsider a decision which will always fill me with regret."

But Hermione, turning slowly, fixed him with her eyes, whose meaning he was farther than ever from understanding, and saying gently, "The matter is at end, Mr. Etheridge," came back to the seat she had vacated, and motioned to him to return to the one he had just left. "Let as talk of other things," said she, and forced her lips to smile.

He obeyed, and at once opened a general conversation. Both sisters joined in it, and such was his influence and the impulse of their own youth that gradually the depth of shadow departed from their faces and a certain grave sort of pleasure appeared there, giving him many a thrill of joy, and making the otherwise dismal hour one to be happily remembered by him through many a weary day and night.

When he came to leave he asked Emma, who strangely enough had now become the most talkative of the two, whether there was not something he could do for her in New York or elsewhere before he came again.

She shook her head, but in another moment, Hermione having stepped aside, she whispered:

"Make my sister smile again as she did a minute ago, and you will give me all the happiness I seek."

The words made him joyous, and the look he bestowed upon her in return had a promise in it which made the young girl's dreams lighter that night, for all the new cause of anxiety which had come into her secluded life.

X.
DORIS.

Frank Etheridge walked musingly towards town. When half-way there he heard his name pronounced behind him in tremulous accents, and turning, saw hastening in his wake the woman who had brought him the message which first took him to Miss Cavanagh's house. She was panting with the haste she had made, and evidently wished to speak to him. He of course stopped, being only too anxious to know what the good woman had to say. She flushed as she came near to him.

"Oh, sir," she cried with an odd mixture of eagerness and restraint, "I have been wanting to talk to you, and if you would be so good as to let me say what is on my mind, it would be a great satisfaction to me, please, and make me feel a deal easier."

"I should be very glad to hear whatever you may have to tell me," was his natural response. "Are you in trouble? Can I help you?"

"Oh, it is not that," she answered, looking about to see if any curious persons were peering at them through the neighboring window-blinds, "though I have my troubles, of course, as who hasn't in this hard, rough world; it is not of myself I want to speak, but of the young ladies. You take an interest in them, sir?"

It was naturally put, yet it made his cheek glow.

"I am their lawyer," he murmured.

"I thought so," she went on as if she had not seen the evidences of emotion on his part, or if she had seen them had failed to interpret them. "Mr. Hamilton is a very good man but he is not of much use, sir; but you look different, as if you could influence them, and make them do as other people do, and enjoy the world, and go out to church, and see the neighbors, and be natural in short."

"And they do not?"

"Never, sir; haven't you heard? They never either of them set foot beyond the garden gate. Miss Emma enjoys the flower-beds and spends most of her time working at them or walking up and down between the poplars, but Miss Hermione keeps to the house and grows white and thin, studying and reading, and making herself wise—for what? No one comes to see them—that is, not often, sir, and when they do, they are stiff and formal, as if the air of the house was chilly with something nobody understood. It isn't right, and it's going against God's laws, for they are both well and able to go about the world as others do. Why, then, don't they do it? That is what I want to know."

"And that is what everybody wants to know," returned Frank, smiling; "but as long as the young ladies do not care to explain themselves I do not see how you or any one else can criticise their conduct. They must have good reasons for their seclusion or they would never deny themselves all the pleasures natural to youth."

"Reasons? What reasons can they have for actions so extraordinary? I don't know of any reason on God's earth which would keep me tied to the house, if my feet were able to travel and my eyes to see."

"Do you live with them?"

"Yes; or how could they get the necessaries of life? I do their marketing, go for the doctor when they are sick, pay their bills, and buy their dresses. That's why their frocks are no prettier," she explained.

Frank felt his wonder increase.

"It is certainly a great mystery," he acknowledged. "I have heard of elderly women showing their eccentricity in this way, but young girls!"

"And such beautiful girls! Do you not think them beautiful?" she asked.

He started and looked at the woman more closely. There was a tone in her voice when she put this question that for the first time made him think that she was less simple than her manner would seem to indicate.

"What is your name?" he asked her abruptly.

"Doris, sir."

"And what is it you want of me?"

"Oh, sir, I thought I told you; to talk to the young ladies and show them how wicked it is to slight the good gifts which the Lord has bestowed upon them. They may listen to you, sir; seeing that you are from out of town and have the ways of the big city about you."

She was very humble now and had dropped her eyes in some confusion at his altered manner, so that she did not see how keenly his glance rested upon her nervous nostril, weak mouth, and obstinate chin. But she evidently felt his sudden distrust, for her hands clutched each other in embarrassment and she no longer spoke with the assurance with which she had commenced the conversation.

"I like the young ladies," she now explained, "and it is for their own good I want them to do differently."

"Have they never been talked to on the subject? Have not their friends or relatives tried to make them break their seclusion?"

"Oh, sir, the times the minister has been to that house! And the doctor telling them they would lose their health if they kept on in the way they were going! But it was all waste breath; they only said they had their reasons, and left people to draw what conclusions they would."

Frank Etheridge, who had a gentleman's instincts, and yet who was too much of a lawyer not to avail himself of the garrulity of another on a question he had so much at heart, stopped, and weighed the matter a moment with himself before he put the one or two questions which her revelations suggested. Should he dismiss the woman with a rebuke for her forwardness, or should he humor her love for talk and learn the few things further which he was in reality burning to hear. His love and interest naturally gained the victory over his pride, and he allowed himself to ask:

"How long have they kept themselves shut up? Is it a year, do you think?"

"Oh, a full year, sir; six months at least before their father died. We did not notice it at first, because they never said anything about it, but at last it became very evident, and then we calculated and found they had not stepped out of the house since the day of the great ball at Hartford."

"The great ball!"

"Yes, sir, a grand party that every one went to. But they did not go, though they had talked about it, and Miss Hermione had her dress ready. And they never went out again, not even to their father's funeral. Think of that, sir, not even to their father's funeral."

"It is very strange," said he, determined at whatever cost to ask Edgar about that ball, and if he went to it.

"And that is not all," continued his now thoroughly reassured companion. "They were never the same girls again after that time. Before then Miss Hermione was the admiration and pride of the whole town, notwithstanding that dreadful scar, while Miss Emma was the life of the house and of every gathering she went into. But afterwards—well, you can see for yourself what they are now; and it was just so before their father died."

Frank longed to ask some questions about this father, but reason bade him desist. He was already humiliating himself enough in thus discussing the daughters with the servant who waited upon them; others must tell him about the old gentleman.

"The house is just like a haunted house," Doris now remarked. Then as she saw him cast her a quick look of renewed interest, she glanced nervously down the street and asked eagerly: "Would you mind turning off into this lane, sir, where there are not so many persons to pry and peer at us? It is still early enough for people to see, and as everybody knows me and everybody by this time must know you, they may wonder to see us talking together, and I do so long to ease my whole conscience now I am about it."

For reply, he took the road she had pointed out. When they were comfortably out of sight from the main street, he stopped again and said:

"What do you mean by haunted?"

"Oh, sir," she began, "not by ghosts; I don't believe in any such nonsense as ghosts; but by memories sir, memories of something which has happened within those four walls and which are now locked up in the hearts of those two girls, making them live like spectres. I am not a fanciful person myself, nor given to imaginings, but that house, especially on nights when the wind blows, seems to be full of something not in nature; and though I do not hear anything or see anything, I feel strange terrors and almost expect the walls to speak or the floors to give up their secrets, but they never do; and that is why I quake in my bed and lie awake so many nights."

"Yet you are not fanciful, nor given to imaginings," smiled Frank.

"No, for there is ground for my secret fears. I see it in the girls' pale looks, I hear it in the girls' restless tread as they pace hour after hour through those lonesome rooms."

"They walk for exercise; they do not use the streets, so they make a promenade of their own floors."

"Do people walk for exercise at night?"

"At *night*?"

"Late at night; at one, two, sometimes three, in the morning? Oh, sir, it is uncanny, I tell you."

"They are not well; lack of change affects their nerves and they cannot sleep, so they walk."

"Very likely, *but they do not walk together*. Sometimes it's one, and sometimes it's the other. I know their different steps, and I never hear them both at the same time."

Frank felt a cold shiver thrill his blood.

"I have been in the house," she resumed, after a minute's pause, "for five years; ever since Mrs. Cavanagh died, and I cannot tell you what its secret is. But it has one, I am certain, and I often go about the halls and into the different rooms and ask low to myself, 'Was it here that it happened, or was it there?' There is a little staircase on the second floor which takes a quick turn towards a big empty room where nobody ever sleeps, and though I have no reason for shuddering at that place, I always do, perhaps because it is in that big room the young ladies walk so much. Can you understand my feeling this way, and I no more than a servant to them?"

A month ago he would have uttered a loud disclaimer, but he had changed much in some regards, so he answered: "Yes, if you really care for them."

The look she gave him proved that she did, beyond all doubt.

"If I did not care for them do you think I would stay in such a gloomy house? I love them both better than anything else in the whole world, and I would not leave them, not for all the money any one could offer me."

She was evidently sincere, and Frank felt a vague relief.

"I am glad," said he, "that they have so good a friend in their own house; as for your fears you will have to bear them, for I doubt if the young ladies will ever take any one into their confidence."

"Not—not their lawyer?"

"No," said he, "not even their lawyer."

She looked disappointed and suddenly very ill at ease.

"I thought you might be masterful," she murmured, "and find out. Perhaps you will some day, and then everything will be different. Miss Emma is the most amiable," said she, "and would not long remain a prisoner if Miss Hermione would consent to leave the house."

"Miss Emma is the younger?"

"Yes, yes, in everything."

"And the sadder!"

"I am not so sure about that, but she shows her feelings plainer, perhaps because her spirits used to be so high."

Frank now felt they had talked long enough, interesting as was the topic on which they were engaged. So turning his face towards the town, he remarked:

"I am going back to New York to-night, but I shall probably be in Marston again soon. Watch well over the young ladies, but do not think of repeating this interview unless something of great importance should occur. It would not please them if they knew you were in the habit of talking them over to me, and it is your duty to act just as they would wish you to."

"I know it, sir, but when it is for their good — —"

"I understand; but let us not repeat it, Doris." And he bade her a kind but significant good-by.

It was now quite dusk, and as he walked towards Dr. Sellick's office, he remembered with some satisfaction that Edgar was usually at home during the early evening. He wanted to talk to him about Hermione's father, and his mood was too impatient for a long delay. He found him as he expected, seated before his desk, and with his·wonted precipitancy dashed at once into his subject.

"Edgar, you told me once that you were acquainted with Miss Cavanagh's father; that you were accustomed to visit him. What kind of a man was he? A hard one?"

Edgar, taken somewhat by surprise, faltered for a moment, but only for a moment.

"I never have attempted to criticise him," said he; "but let me see; he was a straightforward man and a persistent one, never let go when he once entered upon a thing. He could be severe, but I should never have called him hard. He was like—well he was like Raynor, that professor of ours, who understood everything about beetles and butterflies and such small fry, and knew very little about men or their ways and tastes when they did not coincide with his own. Mr. Cavanagh's hobby was not in the line of natural history, but of chemistry, and that is why I visited him so much; we used to experiment together."

"Was it his pastime or his profession? The house does not look as if it had been the abode of a rich man."

"He was not rich, but he was well enough off to indulge his whims. I think he inherited the few thousands, upon the income of which he supported himself and family."

"And he could be severe?"

"Very, if he were interrupted in his work; at other times he was simply amiable and absent-minded. He only seemed to live when he had a retort before him."

"Of what did he die?"

"Apoplexy, I think; I was not here, so do not know the particulars."

"Was he—" Frank turned and looked squarely at his friend, as he always did when he had a venturesome question to put—"was he fond of his daughters?"

Edgar had probably been expecting some such turn in the conversation as this, yet he frowned and answered quite hastily, though with evident conscientiousness:

"I could not make out; I do not know as I ever tried to; the matter did not interest me."

But Frank was bound to have a definite reply.

"I think you will be able to tell me if you will only give your mind to it for a few moments. A father cannot help but show some gleam of affection for two motherless girls."

"Oh, he was proud of them," Edgar hurriedly asserted, "and liked to have them ready to hand him his coffee when his experiments were over; but fond of them in the way you mean, I think not. I imagine they often missed their mother."

"Did you know *her*?"

"No, only as a child. She died when I was a youngster."

"You do not help me much," sighed Frank.

"Help you?"

"To solve the mystery of those girls' lives."

"Oh!" was Edgar's short exclamation.

"I thought I might get at it by learning about the father, but nothing seems to give me any clue."

Edgar rose with a restless air.

"Why not do as I do—let the matter alone?"

"Because," cried Frank, hotly, "my affections are engaged. I love Hermione Cavanagh, and I cannot leave a matter alone that concerns her so nearly."

"I see," quoth Edgar, and became very silent.

When Frank returned to New York it was with the resolution to win the heart of Hermione and then ask her to tell him her secret. He was so sure that whatever it was, it was not one which would stand in the way of his happiness.

XI.
LOVE.

Frank's next business was to read the packet of letters which had been found in old Mrs. Wakeham's bed. The box abstracted by Huckins had been examined during his absence and found to contain securities, which, together with the ready money and papers taken from the clock, amounted to so many thousands that it had become quite a serious matter to find the heir. Huckins still clung to the house, but he gave no trouble. He was satisfied, he said, to abide by the second will, being convinced that if he were patient he would yet inherit through it. His sister Harriet was without doubt dead, and he professed great willingness to give any aid possible in verifying the fact. But as he could adduce no proofs nor suggest any clue to the discovery of this sister's whereabouts if living, or of her grave if dead, his offers were disregarded, and he was allowed to hermitize in the old house undisturbed.

Meantime, false clues came in and false claims were raised by various needy adventurers. To follow up these clues and sift these claims took much of Frank Etheridge's time, and when he was not engaged upon this active work he employed himself in reading those letters to which I have already alluded.

They were of old date and were from various sources. But they conveyed little that was likely to be of assistance to him. Of the twenty he finally read, only one was signed Harriet, and while that was very interesting to him, as giving some glimpses into the early history of this woman, it did not give him any facts upon which either he or the police could work. I will transcribe the letter here:

"My Dear Cynthia:

"You are the only one of the family to whom I dare write. I have displeased father too much to ever hope for his forgiveness, while mother will never go against his wishes, even if the grief of it should make me die. I am very unhappy, I can tell you that, more unhappy than even they could wish, but they must never know it, never. I have still enough pride to wish to keep my misery to myself, and it would be just the one thing that would make my burden unbearable, to have them know I regretted the marriage on account of which I have been turned away from their hearts and home forever. But I do regret it, Cynthia, from the bottom of my heart. He is not kind, and he is not a gentleman, and I made a terrible mistake, as you can see. But I do not think I was to blame. He seemed so devoted, and used to make me such beautiful speeches that I never thought to ask if he were a good man; and when father and mother opposed him so bitterly that we had to meet by stealth, he was always so considerate, and yet so determined, that he seemed to me like an angel till we were married, and then it was too late to do anything but accept my fate. I think he expected father to forgive us and take us home, and when he found these expectations false he became both ugly and sullen, and so my life is nothing but a burden to me, and I almost wish I was dead. But I am very strong, and so is he, and so we are likely to live on, pulling away at the chain that binds us, till both are old and gray.

"Pretty talk for a young girl's reading, is it not? But it relieves me to pour out my heart to some one that loves me, and I know that you do. But I shall never talk like this to you again or ever write you another letter. You are my father's darling, and I want you to remain so, and if you think too much of me, or spend your time in writing to me, he will find it out, and that will help neither of us. So good-by, little Cynthia, and do not be angry that I put a false address at the top of the page, or refuse to tell you where I live, or where I am going. From this hour Harriet is dead to you, and nothing shall ever induce me to break the silence which should remain between us but my meeting you in another world, where all the follies of this will be forgotten in the love that has survived both life and death.

"Your sorrowing but true sister,

"Harriet."

The date was forty years back, and the address was New York City—an address which she acknowledged to be false. The letter was without envelope.

The only other allusion to this sister found in the letters was in a short note written by a person called Mary, and it ran thus:

"Do you know whom I have seen? Your sister Harriet. It was in the depot at New Haven. She was getting off the train and I was getting on, but I knew her at once for all the change which ten years make in the most of us, and catching her by the arm, I cried, 'Harriet, Harriet, where are you living?' How she blushed and what a start she gave! but as soon as she saw who it was she answered readily enough, 'In Marston,' and disappeared in the crowd before I could say another word. Wasn't it a happy chance, and isn't it a relief to know she is alive and well. As for her looks, they were quite lively, and she wore nice clothing like one in very good circumstances. So you see her marriage did not turn out as badly as some thought."

This was of old date also, and gave no clue to the sender, save such as was conveyed by the signature Mary. Mary what? Mr. Huckins was the only person who was likely to know.

Frank, who had but little confidence in this man and none in his desire to be of use in finding the legal heir, still thought it best to ask him if there was any old friend of the family whose first name was Mary. So he went to Flatbush one afternoon, and finding the old miser in his house, put to him this question and waited for his reply.

It came just as he expected, with a great show of willingness that yet was without any positive result.

"Mary? Mary?" he repeated, "we have known a dozen Marys. Do you mean any one belonging to this town?"

"I mean some one with whom your sister was intimate thirty years ago. Some one who knew your other sister, the one who married Smith; some one who would simply sign her first name in writing to Mrs. Wakeham, and who in speaking of Mrs. Smith would call her Harriet."

"Ah!" ejaculated the cautious Huckins, dropping his eyes for fear they would convey more than his tongue might deem fit. "I'm afraid I was too young in those days to know much about my sister's friends. Can you tell me where she lived, or give me any information beyond her first name by which I could identify her?"

"No," was the lawyer's quick retort; "if I could I should not need to consult you; I could find the woman myself."

"Ah, I see, I see, and I wish I could help you, but I really don't know whom you mean, I don't indeed, sir. May I ask where you got the name, and why you want to find the woman?"

"Yes, for it involves your prospects. This Mary, whoever she may have been, was the one to tell Mrs. Wakeham that Harriet Smith lived in Marston. Doesn't that jog your memory, Huckins? You know you cannot inherit the property till it is proved that Harriet is dead and left no heirs."

"I know," he whined, and looked quite disconsolate, but he gave the lawyer no information, and Frank left at last with the feeling that he had reached the end of his rope.

As a natural result, his thoughts turned to Marston—were they ever far away from there? "I will go and ease my heart of some of its burden," thought he; "perhaps my head may be clearer then, and my mind freer for work." Accordingly he took the train that day, and just as the dew of evening began to fall, he rode into Marston and stopped at Miss Cavanagh's door.

He found Hermione sitting at an old harp. She did not seem to have been playing but musing, and her hands hung somewhat listlessly upon the strings. As she rose the instrument gave out a thrilling wail that woke an echo in his sensibilities for which he was not prepared. He had considered himself in a hopeful frame of mind, and behold, he was laboring instead under a morbid fear that his errand would be in vain. Emma was not present, but another lady was, whose aspect of gentle old age was so sweet and winning that he involuntarily bent his head in reverence to her, before Hermione could utter the introduction which was trembling on her tongue.

"My father's sister," said she, "and our very dear aunt. She is quite deaf, so she would not hear you speak if you attempted it, but she reads faces wonderfully, and you see she is smiling at you as she does not smile at every one. You may consider yourself introduced."

Frank, who had a tender heart for all misfortune, surveyed the old lady wistfully. How placid she looked, how at home with her thoughts! It was peacefulness to the spirit to meet her eye. Bowing again, he turned towards Hermione and remarked:

"What a very lovely face! She looks as if she had never known anything but the pleasures of life."

"On the contrary," returned Hermione, "she has never known much but its disappointments. But they have left no trace on her face, or in her nature, I think. She is an embodiment of trust, and in the great silence there is about her, she hears sounds and sees visions which are denied to others. But when did you come to Marston?"

He told her he had just arrived, and, satisfied with the slight look of confusion which mantled her face at this acknowledgment, launched into talk all tending to one end, his love for her. But he did not reach that end immediately; for if the old lady could not hear, she could see, and Frank, for all his impetuosity, possessed sufficient restraint upon himself not to subject himself or Hermione to the criticism of even this most benignant relative. Not till Mrs. Lovell left the room, as she did after a while,—being a very wise old lady as well as mild,—did he allow himself to say:

"There can be but one reason now for my coming to Marston—to see you, Miss Cavanagh; I have no other business here."

"I thought," she began, with some confusion,—evidently she had been taken by surprise,—"that you were looking for some one, a Harriet Smith, I think, whom you had reason to believe once lived here."

"I did come to Marston originally on that errand, but I have so far failed in finding any trace of her in this place that I begin to think we were mistaken in our inferences that she had ever lived here."

"Yet you had reason for thinking that she did," Hermione went on, with the anxiety of one desirous to put off the declaration she probably saw coming.

"Yes; we had reasons, but they prove to have been unfounded."

"Was—was your motive for finding her an important one?" she asked, with some hesitation, and a look of curiosity in her fine eyes.

"Quite; a fortune of some thousands is involved in her discovery. She is heiress to at least a hundred thousand dollars from a sister she has not seen since they were girls together."

"Indeed!" and Hermione's eyes opened in some surprise, then fell before the burning light in his.

"But do not let us talk of a matter that for me is now of secondary interest," cried he, letting the full stream of his ardor find its way. "You are all I can think of now; you, you, whom I have loved since I caught the first glimpse of your face one night through the window yonder. Though I have known you but a little while, and though I cannot hope to have awakened a kindred feeling in you, you have so filled my mind and heart during the few short weeks since I learned your name, that I find it impossible to keep back the words which the sight of your face calls forth. I love you, and I want to guard you from loneliness forever. Will you give me that sweet right?"

"But," she cried, starting to her feet in an excitement that made her face radiantly beautiful, "you do not seem to think of my misfortune, my——"

"Do you mean this scar?" he whispered softly, gliding swiftly to her side. "It is no misfortune in my eyes; on the contrary, I think it endears you to me all the more. I love it, Hermione, because it is a part of you. See how I feel towards it!" and he bent his head with a quick movement, and imprinted a kiss upon the mark she had probably never touched herself but with shrinking.

"Oh!" went up from her lips in a low cry, and she covered her face with her hands in a rush of feeling that was not entirely connected with that moment.

"Did you think I would let that stand in my way?" he asked, with a proud tenderness with which no sensitive woman could fail to be impressed. "It is one reason more for a man to love your beautiful face, your noble manners, your soft white hand. I think half the pleasure would be gone from the prospect of loving you if I did not hope to make you forget what you have perhaps too often remembered."

She dropped her hands, and he saw her eyes fixed upon him with a strange look.

"O how wicked I have been!" she murmured. "And what good men there are in the world!"

He shook his head.

"It is not goodness," he began, but she stopped him with a wave of her hand.

A strange elation seemed to have taken hold of her, and she walked the floor with lifted head and sparkling eye.

"It restores my belief in love," she exclaimed, "and in mankind." And she seemed content just to brood upon that thought.

But he was not; naturally he wished for some assurance from her; so he stepped in her path as she was crossing the room, and, taking her by the hands, said, smilingly:

"Do you know how you can testify your appreciation in a way to make me perfectly happy?"

She shook her head, and tried to draw her hands away.

"By taking a walk, the least walk in the world, beyond that wooden gate."

She shuddered and her hands fell from his.

"You do not know what you ask," said she; then after a moment, "it was that I meant and not the scar, when I spoke of my misfortune. I cannot go outside the garden wall, and I was wrong to listen to your words for a moment, knowing what a barrier this fact raises up between us."

"Hermione,—" he was very serious now, and she gathered up all her strength to meet the questions she knew were coming,—"why cannot you go beyond the garden gate? Cannot you tell me? Or do you hesitate because you are afraid I shall smile at your reasons for this determined seclusion?"

"I am not afraid of your smiling, but I cannot give my reasons. That I consider them good must answer for us both."

"Very well, then, we will let them answer. You need not take the walk I ask, but give me instead another pleasure—your promise to be my wife."

"Your wife?"

"Yes, Hermione."

"With such a secret between us?"

"It will not be a secret long."

"Mr. Etheridge," she cried with emotion, "you do not know the woman you thus honor. If it had been Emma——"

"It is you I love."

"It would have been safe," she went on as if she had not heard him. "She is lovely, and amiable, and constant, and in her memory there is no dark scar as there is in mine, a scar deeper than this," she said, laying her finger on her cheek, "and fully as ineffaceable."

"Some day you will take me into your confidence," he averred, "and then that scar will gradually disappear."

"What confidence you have in me?" she cried. "What have you seen, what can you see in me to make you trust me so in face of my own words?"

"I think it is the look in your eyes. There is purity there, Hermione, and a deep sadness which is too near like sorrow to be the result of an evil action."

"What do you call evil?" she cried. Then suddenly, "I once did a great wrong—in a fit of temper—and I can never undo it, never, yet its consequences are lasting. Would you give your heart to a woman who could so forget herself, and who is capable of forgetting herself again if her passions are roused as they were then?"

"Perhaps not," he acknowledged, "but my heart is already given and I do not know how to take it back."

"Yet you must," said she. "No man with a career before him should marry a recluse, and I am that, whatever else I may or may not be. I would be doing a second ineffaceable wrong if I took advantage of your generous impulse and bound you to a fate that in less than two months would be intolerably irksome to one of your temperament."

"Now you do not know me," he protested.

But she heeded neither his words nor his pleading look.

"I know human nature," she avowed, "and if I do not mingle much with the world I know the passions that sway it. I can never be the wife of any man, Mr. Etheridge, much less of one so generous and so self-forgetting as yourself."

"Do you—are you certain?" he asked.

"Certain."

"Then I have not succeeded in raising one throb of interest in your breast?"

She opened her lips and his heart stood still for her answer, but she closed them again and remained standing so long with her hands locked together and her face downcast, that his hopes revived again, and he was about to put in another plea for her hand when she looked up and said firmly:

"I think you ought to know that my heart does not respond to your suit. It may make any disappointment which you feel less lasting."

He uttered a low exclamation and stepped back.

"I beg your pardon," said he, "I ought not to have annoyed you. You will forget my folly, I hope."

"Do you forget it!" cried she; but her lips trembled and he saw it.

"Hermione! Hermione!" he murmured, and was down at her feet before she could prevent it. "Oh, how I love you!" he breathed, and kissed her hand wildly, passionately.

XII.
HOW MUCH DID IT MEAN?

Frank Etheridge left the presence of Hermione Cavanagh, carrying with him an indelible impression of her slender, white-robed figure and pallid, passion-drawn face. There was such tragedy in the latter, that he shuddered at its memory, and stopped before he reached the gate to ask himself if the feeling she displayed was for him or another. If for another, then was that other Dr. Sellick, and as the name formed itself in his thoughts, he felt the dark cloud of jealousy creep over his mind, obscuring the past and making dangerous the future.

"How can I know," thought he, "how can I know?" and just as the second repetition passed his lips, he heard a soft step near him, and, looking up, saw the gentle Emma watering her flowers.

To gain her side was his first impulse. To obtain her confidence the second. Taking the heavy watering-pot from her hand, he poured its contents on the rose-bush she was tending, and then setting it down, said quietly:

"I have just made your sister very unhappy, Miss Cavanagh."

She started and her soft eyes showed the shadow of an alarm.

"I thought you were her friend," she said.

He drew her around the corner of the house towards the poplar trees. "Had I been only that," he avowed, "I might have spared her pain, but I am more than that, Miss Cavanagh, I am her lover."

The hesitating step at his side paused, and though no great change came into her face, she seemed to have received a shock.

"I can understand," said she, "that you hurt her."

"Is she so wedded to the past, then?" he cried. "Was there some one, is there some one whom she—she——"

He could not finish, but the candid-eyed girl beside him did not profess to misunderstand him. A pitiful smile crossed her lips, and she looked for a minute whiter than her sister had done, but she answered firmly:

"You could easily overcome any mere memory, but the decision she has made never to leave the house, I fear you cannot overcome."

"Does it spring—forgive me if I go beyond the bounds of discretion, but this mystery is driving me mad—does it spring from that past attachment you have almost acknowledged?"

She drooped her head and his heart misgave him. Why should he hurt both these women when his whole feeling towards them was one of kindness and love?

"Pardon me," he pleaded. "I withdraw the question; I had no right to put it."

"Thank you," said she, and looked away from him towards the distant prospect of hill and valley lying before them.

He stood revolving the matter in his disturbed mind.

"I should have been glad to have been the means of happiness to your sister and yourself. Such seclusion as you have imposed upon yourselves seems unnecessary, but if it must be, and this garden wall is destined to be the boundary of your world, it would have been a great pleasure to me to have brought into it some freshness from the life which lies beyond it. But it is destined not to be."

The sad expression in her face changed into one of wistfulness.

"Then you are not coming any more?" said she.

He caught his breath. There was disappointment in her tones and this could mean nothing but regret, and regret meant the loss of something which might have been hope. She felt, then, that he might have won her sister if he had been more patient.

"Do you think it will do for me to come here after your sister has told me that it was useless for me to aspire to her hand?"

She gave him for the first time a glance that had the element of mirthfulness in it.

"Come as my friend," she suggested; then in a more serious mood added: "It is her only chance of happiness, but I do not know that I would be doing right in influencing you to pursue a suit which may not be for yours. *You* know, or will know after reflection (and I advise you to reflect well), whether an alliance with women situated as we are would be conducive to your welfare. If you decide yes, think that a woman taken by surprise, as my sister undoubtedly was, may not in the first hurried moment of decision know her own mind, but also remember that no woman who has taken such a decision as she has, is cast in the common mould, and that you may but add to your regrets by a persistency she may never fully reward."

Astonished at her manner and still more astonished at the intimation conveyed in her last words, he looked at her as one who would say:

"But you also share her fate and the resolve that made it."

She seemed to understand him.

"Free Hermione," she whispered, "from the shackles she has wound about herself and you will free me."

"Miss Emma," he began, but she put her finger on her lips.

"Hush!" she entreated; "let us not talk any more about it. I have already said what I never meant should pass my lips; but the affection I bear my sister made me forget myself; she does so need to love and be loved."

"And you think I——"

"Ah, sir, you must be the judge of your own chances. You have heard her refusal and must best know just how much it means."

"How much it means!" Long did Frank muse over that phrase, after he had left the sweet girl who had uttered it. As he sat with Edgar at supper, his abstracted countenance showed that he was still revolving the question, though he endeavored to seem at home with his friend and interested in the last serious case which had occupied the attention of the newly settled doctor. How much it means! Not much, he was beginning to say to himself, and insensibly his face began to brighten and his manner to grow less restrained, when Edgar, who had been watching him furtively, broke out:

"Now you are more like yourself. Business responsibilities are as hard to shake off as a critical case in medicine."

"Yes," was the muttered reply, as Frank rose from the table, and took the cigar his friend offered him. "And business with me just now is particularly perplexing. I cannot get any clue to Harriet Smith or her heirs, nor can the police or the presumably sharp detective I have put upon the search."

"That must please Huckins."

"Yes, confound him! such a villain as he is! I sometimes wonder if he killed his sister."

"That you can certainly find out."

"No, for she had a mortal complaint, and that satisfies the physicians. But there are ways of hastening a death, and those I dare avow he would not be above using. The greed in his eyes would do anything; it even suffices to make him my very good friend, now that he sees that he might lose everything by opposing me."

"I am glad you see through his friendship."

"See through a sieve?"

"He plays his part badly, then?"

"He cannot help it, with that face of his; and then he gave himself away in the beginning. No attitude he could take now would make me forget the sneak I saw in him then."

This topic was interesting, but Edgar knew it was no matter of business which had caused the fitful changes he had been observing in Frank's tell-tale countenance. Yet he did not broach any other theme, and it was Frank who finally remarked:

"I suppose you think me a fool to fix my heart on a woman with a secret."

"Fool is a strong word," answered Edgar, somewhat bitterly, "but that you were unfortunate to have been attracted by Hermione Cavanagh, I think any man would acknowledge. You would acknowledge it yourself, if you stopped to weigh the consequences of indulging a passion for a woman so eccentric."

"Perhaps I should, if my interest would allow me to stop. But it won't, Edgar; it has got too strong a hold upon me; everything else sinks in importance before it. I love her, and am willing to sacrifice something for her sake."

"Something, perhaps; but in this case it would be everything."

"I do not think so."

"You do not think so now; but you would soon."

"Perhaps I should, but it is hard to realize it. Besides, she would drop her eccentricities if her affections once became engaged."

"Oh, if you have assurance of that."

"Do I need assurance? Doesn't it stand to reason? A woman loved is so different from a woman — —" scorned, he was going to say, but, remembering himself, added softly, "from a woman who has no one to think of but herself."

"This woman has a sister," observed Edgar.

Frank faltered. "Yes, and that sister is involved in her fate," thought he, but he said, quietly: "Emma Cavanagh does not complain of Hermione; on the contrary, she expresses the greatest affection for her."

"They are both mysteries," exclaimed Edgar, and dropped the subject, though it was not half talked out.

Frank was quite willing to accept his silence, for he was out of sorts with his friend and with himself. He knew his passion was a mad one, and yet he felt that it had made giant strides that day, and had really been augmented instead of diminished by the refusal he had received from Hermione, and the encouragement to persistence which he had received from her usually shy sister. As the evening wore on and the night approached, his thoughts not only grew in intensity, but deepened into tenderness. It was undoubtedly a passion that had smitten him, but that passion was hallowed by the unselfish feelings of a profound affection. He did not want her to engage herself to him if it would not be for her happiness. That it would be, every throb of his heart assured him, but he might be mistaken, and if so, better her dreams of the past than a future he could not make bright. He was so moved at the turmoil which his thoughts made in his usually quiet breast, that he could not think of sleep, but sat in his room for hours indulging in dreams which his practical nature would have greatly scorned a few short weeks before. He saw her again in fancy in every attitude in which his eyes had ever beheld her, and sanctified thus by distance, her beauty seemed both wonderful and touching. And that was not all. Some chord between them seemed to have been struck, and he felt himself drawn towards her as if (it was a strange fancy) she stood by that garden gate, and was looking in his direction with rapt, appealing eyes. So strong became that fancy at last, that he actually rose to his feet and went to the window which opened towards the south.

"Hermione! Hermione!" broke in longing from his lips, and then annoyed at what he could not but consider a display of weakness on his part, he withdrew himself from the window, determined to forget for the moment that there lived for him such a cause for love and sorrow. But what man can forget by a mere effort of will, or what lover shut his eyes to the haunting vision which projects itself upon the inner consciousness. In fancy he saw her still, and this time she seemed to be pacing up and down the poplar walk, wringing her hands and wildly calling his name. It was more than he could bear. He must know if this was only an hallucination, and in a feverish impulse he rushed from his room with the intention of going to her at once.

But he no sooner stood in the hall than he realized he was not alone in the house, and that he should have to pass Edgar's door. He naturally felt some hesitation at this and was inclined to give up his purpose. But the fever urging him on said no; so stealing warily down the hall he stepped softly by the threshold of his friend's room, when to his surprise he perceived that the door was ajar.

Pushing it gently open he found the room brilliant with moonlight but empty. Greatly relieved and considering that the doctor had been sent for by some suffering patient, he passed at once out of the house.

He went directly to that of Hermione, walking where the shadows were thickest as if he were afraid of being recognized. But no one was in the streets, and when he reached the point where the tall poplar-trees made a wall against the moonbeams, he slid into the deep obscurity he found there with a feeling of relief such as the heart experiences when it is suddenly released from some great strain.

Was she in the poplar walk? He did not mean to accost her if she were, nor to show himself or pass beyond the boundary of the wall, but he must know if her restless spirit drove her to pace these moonlit walks, and if it were true or not that she was murmuring his name.

The gate which opened in the wall at the side of the house was in a direct line with the window he had long ago fixed upon as hers. He accordingly took up his station at that spot and as he did so he was sure that he saw the flitting of some dark form amid the alternate bands of moonlight and shadow that lay across the weird pathway before him. Holding his breath he listened. Oh, the stillness of the night! How awesome and yet how sweet it was! But is there no break in the universal silence? Above his head the ever restless leaves make a low murmuring, and far away in the dim distances rises a faint sound that he cannot mistake; it is the light footfall of a dainty woman.

He can see her now. She is coming towards him, her shadow gliding before her. Seeing it he quails. From the rush of emotion seizing him, he knows that he should not be upon this spot, and panting with the effort, he turns and flees just as the sudden sound of a lifted window comes from the house.

That arrests him. Pausing, he looks up. It is her window that is open, and in the dark square thus made he sees her face bright with the moonlight streaming over it. Instantly he recovers himself. It is Emma's step, not Hermione's, he hears upon the walk. Hermione is above and in an anxious mood, for she is looking eagerly out and calling her sister by name.

"I am coming," answers back the clear, low voice of Emma from below.

"It is late," cries Hermione, "and very cold. Come in, Emma."

"I am coming," repeated the young girl. And in another moment he heard her step draw nearer, saw her flitting figure halt for a moment on the doorstep before him and then disappear just as the window closed above. He had not been observed.

Relieved, he drew a long breath and leaned his head against the garden wall. Ah, how fair had been the vision of his beloved one's face in the moonlight. It filled him with indescribable thoughts; it made his spirit reel and his heart burn; it made him ten times her lover. Yet because he was her lover he felt that he ought not to linger there any longer; that the place was hallowed even from his presence, and that he should return at once to the doctor's house. But when he lifted his head he heard steps, this time not within the wall but on the roadside behind him, and alert at once to the mischievous surmises which might be aroused by the discovery of his presence there, he remained perfectly still in the hope that his form would be so lost in the deep shadows where he had withdrawn himself, that he would not be seen.

But the person, whoever it was, had evidently already detected him, for the footsteps turned the corner and advanced rapidly to where he stood. Should he step forward and meet the intruder, or remain still and await the words of surprise he had every reason to expect? He decided to remain where he was, and in another moment realized his wisdom in doing so, for the footsteps passed on and did not halt till they had reached the gate. But they paused there and at once he felt himself seized by a sudden jealousy and took a step forward, eager to see what this man would do.

He did not do much; he cast a look up at the house, and a heavy sigh broke from his lips; then he leaned forward and plucked a rose that grew inside the wall and kissed it there in the moonlight, and put it inside his breast-pocket; then he turned again towards the highway, and started back in surprise to see Frank Etheridge standing before him.

"Edgar!" cried the one.

"Frank!" exclaimed the other.

"You have misled me," accused Frank; "you do love her, or you would not be here."

"Love whom?" asked Edgar, bitterly.

"Hermione."

"Does Hermione tend the flowers?"

"Ah!" ejaculated Frank, understanding his friend for the first time; "it is Emma you are attached to. I see! I see! Forgive me, Edgar; passion is so blind to everything but its own object. Of course it is Emma; why shouldn't it be!"

Yet for all its assurance his voice had strange tones in it, and Edgar, already annoyed at his own self-betrayal, looked at him suspiciously as they drew away together towards the main street.

"I am glad to find this out," said Frank, with a hilarity slightly forced, or so thought his friend, who could not know what thoughts and hopes this discovery had awakened in the other's breast. "You have kept your secret well, but now that I know it you cannot refuse to make me your confidant, when there is so much to tell involving my happiness as well as your own."

"I have no happiness, Frank."

"Nor I; but I mean to have."

"Mean to marry Miss Cavanagh?"

"Of course, if I can induce her to marry me."

"I do not mean to marry Emma."

"You do not? Because she has a secret? because she is involved in a mystery?"

"Partly; that would be enough, Frank; but I have another good reason. Miss Emma Cavanagh does not care for me."

"You know that? You have asked her?"

"A year ago; this is no sudden passion with me; I have loved her all my life."

"Edgar! And you mean to give her up?"

"Give her up?"

"If I were you, nothing would induce me to resign my hopes, not even her own coldness. I *would* win her. Have you tried again since your return?"

"Frank, she is a recluse now; I could not marry a recluse; my wife must play her part in the world, and be my helpmate abroad as well as at home."

"Yes, yes; but as I said in my own case, win her love and that will all right itself. No woman's resolve will hold out against a true passion."

"But you forget, she has no true passion for me."

Frank did not answer; he was musing over the subject. He had had an opportunity for seeing into the hearts of these girls which had been denied to Edgar. Had he seen love there? Yes, but in Hermione's breast, not Emma's. And yet Emma was deeply sad, and it was Emma whom he had just seen walking her restlessness off under the trees at midnight.

"Edgar," he suddenly exclaimed, "you may not understand this girl. Their whole existence is a mystery, and so may their hearts be. Won't you tell me how it was she refused you? It may serve to throw some light upon the facts."

"What light? She refused me as all coquettish women refuse the men whom they have led to believe in their affection."

"Ah! you once believed, then, in her affection."

"Should I have offered myself if I had not?"

"I don't know; I only know I didn't wait for any such belief on the part of Hermione."

"You are impulsive, Frank, I am not; I weigh well what I do, fortunately for myself."

"Yet you did not prosper in this affair."

"No, because I did not take a woman's waywardness into consideration. I thought I had a right to count upon her regard, and I found myself mistaken."

"Explain yourself," entreated Frank.

"Will not to-morrow do? Here we are at home, and it must be one o'clock at least."

"I should sleep better if I knew it all now," Frank intimated.

"Well, then, come to my room; but there is nothing in the story to specially interest you. I loved her — —"

"Edgar, you must be explicit. I am half lawyer in listening to this tale; I want to understand these girls."

"Girls? It is of Emma only that I have to speak."

"I know, but tell the story with some details; tell me where you first met her."

"Oh, if I must," sighed Edgar, who hated all talk about himself, "let's be comfortable." And throwing himself into a chair, he pointed out another to Frank.

"This is more like it," acknowledged the latter.

Edgar lit a cigar; perhaps he felt that he could hide all emotion behind its fumes. Frank did not take one.

"I have known Emma Cavanagh ever since we were children," began Edgar. "As a school-boy I thought her the merriest-eyed witch in town. — — Is she merry now?"

Frank shook his head.

"Well, I suppose she has grown older, but then she was as full of laughter and fun as any blue-eyed Mischief could well be, and I, who have a cynical turn of mind, liked the brightness of hers as I shall never like her sadness—if she is sad. But that was in my adolescence, and being as shy as I was inclined to be cynical, I never showed her my preference, or even joined the mirthful company of which she was the head. I preferred to stand back and hear her laughter, or talk to Hermione while watching her sister."

"Ah!" thought Frank.

"When I went to college she went to school, and when I graduated as a doctor she was about graduating also. But she did not come home at that time for more than a fleeting visit. Friends wished her company on a trip abroad, and she went away from Marston just as I settled here for my first year of practice. I was disappointed at this, but I made what amends to myself I could by cultivating the acquaintance of her father, and making myself necessary to him by my interest in his studies. I spent much of my spare time at the house, and though I never asked after Emma, I used to get continual news of her from her sister."

"Ah!" again ejaculated Frank to himself.

"At last she returned, and—I do not know how she looks now, but she was pretty then, wonderfully pretty, and more animated in her manner than any other woman I have ever seen. I saw her first at a picnic, and though I lacked courage to betray the full force of my feeling, I imagined she understood me, for her smiles became dazzling, and she joked with everybody but me. At last I had her for a few minutes to myself, and then the pent up passion of months had its way, and I asked her to be my wife. Frank, you may find it easy to talk about these things, but I do not. I can only say she seemed to listen to me with modest delight, and when I asked her for her answer she gave me a look I shall never forget, and would have spoken but that her father called her just then, and we were obliged to separate. I saw her for just another moment that day, but there were others about, and I could only whisper, 'If you love me, come to the ball next week'; to which she gave me no other reply than an arch look and a smile which, as I have said before, appeared to promise me all I could desire. Appeared, but did not; for when I called at the house the next day I was told that Mr. Cavanagh was engaged in an experiment that could not be interrupted, and when I asked to see the ladies received word that they were very busy preparing for the ball and could see no one. Relieved at this, for the ball was near at hand, I went home, and being anxious to do the honorable thing, I wrote to Mr. Cavanagh, and, telling him that I loved his daughter, formally asked for the honor of her hand. This note I sent by a messenger.

"I did not receive an immediate reply (why do you want all these particulars, Frank?); but I did not worry, for her look was still warm in my memory. But when two days passed and no message arrived I became uneasy, and had it not been for the well-known indifference of Mr. Cavanagh to all affairs of life outside of his laboratory, I should have given up in despair. But as it was, I kept my courage up till the night of the ball, when it suddenly fell, never to rise again. For will you believe it, Frank, she was not there, nor any of her family, though all had engaged to go, and had made many preparations for the affair, as I knew."

"And did no letter come? Did you never see Miss Cavanagh again, or any of her family?"

"I received a note, but it was very short, though it was in Emma's handwriting. She had not been well, was her excuse, and so could not be present at the ball. As for the offer I had been kind enough to make her, it was far above her deserts, and so must be gratefully declined. Then came a burst of something like contrition, and the prayer that I would not seek to make her alter her mind, as her decision was irrevocable. Added to this was one line from her father, to the effect that interesting as our studies were, he felt compelled to tell me he should have no further time to give to them at present, and so bade me a kindly adieu. Was there ever a more complete dismissal? I felt as if I had been thrust out of the house."

Frank, who was nothing if not sympathetic, nodded quickly, but did not break into those open expressions of indignation which his friend had evidently anticipated. The truth was, he was too busy considering the affair, and asking himself what part Hermione had taken in it, and whether all its incongruities were not in some way due to her. He was so anxious to assure himself that this was not so, that he finally asked:

"And was that the end? Did you never see any of them again?"

"I did not wish to," was the answer. "I had already thought of trying my fortunes in the West, and when this letter came, it determined me. In three weeks I had left Marston as I thought forever, but I was not successful in the West."

"And you will be here," observed Frank.

"I think so," said Edgar, and became suddenly silent.

Frank looked at him a long time and then said quietly:

"I am glad you love her still."

Edgar, flushing, opened his lips, but the other would not listen to any denial.

"If you had not loved her, you would not have come back to Marston, and if you did not love her still, you would not pluck roses from her wall at midnight."

"I was returning from a patient," objected Edgar, shortly.

"I know, but you *stopped*. You need not blush to own it, for, as I say, I think it a good thing that you have not forgotten Miss Cavanagh." And not being willing to explain himself further, Frank rose and sauntered towards the door. "We have talked well into the night," he remarked; "supposing we let up now, and continue our conversation to-morrow."

"I am willing to let up," acquiesced Edgar, "but why continue to-morrow? Nothing can be gained by fruitless conjectures on this subject, while much peace of mind may be lost by them."

"Well, perhaps you are right," quoth Frank.

XIII.
FRESH DOUBTS.

Frank was recalled to business the next day by the following letter from Flatbush:

Dear Mr. Etheridge:

It has been discovered this afternoon that Mr. Huckins has left town. When he went or where he has gone, no one seems to know. Indeed, it was supposed that he was still in the house, where he has been hiding ever since the investigations were over, but a neighbor, having occasion to go in there to-day, found the building empty, and all of Mr. Huckins' belongings missing. I thought you would like to know of this disappearance.

Yours truly,

A. W. Seney.

As this was an affair for the police, Frank immediately returned to New York; but it was not many days before he was back again in Marston, determined to see Miss Cavanagh once more, and learn if his suit was as really hopeless as it appeared. He brought a box of some beautiful orchids with him, and these he presented to Miss Emma as being the one most devoted to flowers.

Hermione looked a little startled at his presence, but Mrs. Lovell, the dear old lady who was paying them a visit, smiled gently upon him, and he argued well from that smile, knowing that it was not without its meaning from one whose eyes were so bright with intelligence as her's.

The evening was cool for summer, and a fire had been lighted in the grate. By this fire they all sat and Frank, who was strangely happy, entertained the three recluses with merry talk which was not without a hidden meaning for one of the quiet listeners. When the old aunt rose and slipped away, the three drew nearer, and the conversation became more personal. At last—how was it done—Emma vanished also, and Frank, turning to utter some witty speech, found only Hermione's eyes confronting him in the fire-glow. At once the words faltered on his tongue, and leaning forward he reached out his hand, for she was about to rise also.

"Do not rob me of this one moment," he prayed. "I have come back, you see, because I could not stay away. Say that it does not anger you; say that I may come now and then and see your face, even if I may not hope for all that my heart craves."

"Do I look angry?" she asked, with a sad smile.

"No," he whispered; "nor do you look glad."

"Glad," she murmured, "glad"; and the bitterness in her tone revealed to him how strong were the passions that animated her. "I have no business with gladness, not even if my own fate changed. I have forfeited all joy, Mr. Etheridge; and that I thought you understood."

"You speak like one who has committed a crime," he smiled; "nothing else should make you feel as you do."

She started and her eyes fell. Then they rose suddenly and looked squarely into his. "There are other crimes than those which are marked by blood," said she. "Perhaps I am not altogether guiltless."

Frank shuddered; he had expected her to repel the charge which he had only made in the hopes of showing her into what a morbid condition she had fallen.

"My hands are clean," she went on, "but my soul is in shadow. Why did you make me speak of it? You are my friend and I want to keep your friendship, but you see why it must not grow into love; *must not* I say, for both our sakes. It would be fatal."

"I do not see that," he cried impetuously. "You do not make me see it. You hint and assert, but you tell me nothing. You should give me facts, Hermione, and then I could judge whether I should go or stay."

She flushed, and her face, which had been lifted to his, slowly sank.

"You do not know what you ask of me," she murmured.

"I know that I have asked you to be my wife."

"And it was generous of you, very generous. Such generosity merits confidence, but—Let us talk of something else," she cried. "I am not fit—not well enough, I mean, to speak of serious matters to-night. Tell me about your affairs. Tell me if you have found Harriet Smith."

"No," he returned, greatly disappointed, for there had been something like yielding in her manner a moment before. "There is no Harriet Smith, and I do not even know that there is a Hiram Huckins, for he too has disappeared and cannot be found."

"Hiram Huckins?"

"Yes, her brother and the brother of Mrs. Wakeham, whose will has made all this trouble. He is the heir who will inherit her property if Harriet Smith or her children cannot be found, and as the latter contingency is not likely to happen, it is odd that he should have run away without letting us know where he can be found."

"Is he a good man?"

"Hardly. Indeed I consider him a rascal; but he has a good claim on the property, as I have already said, and that is what angers me. A hundred thousand dollars should not fall into the hands of one so mean and selfish as he is."

"Poetic justice is not always shown in this world. Perhaps if you found the true heirs, you would find them also lacking in much that was admirable."

"Possibly; but they would not be apt to be as bad as he is."

"Is he dishonest?"

"I do not like to accuse him, but neither would I like to trust him with another man's money."

"That is unfortunate," said she. "And he will really have this money if you do not find any nearer heirs?"

"Certainly; his name follows theirs in the will."

"It is a pity," she observed, rising and moving towards the harp. "Do you want to hear a song that Emma composed when we were happier than we are now?"

"Indeed I do," was his eager reply. "Sing, I entreat you, sing; it will make me feel as if the gloom was lifting from between us."

But at this word, she came quickly back and sat down in her former place by the fire.

"I do not know what came over me," said she; "I never sing." And she looked with a severe and sombre gaze into the flames before her.

"Hermione, have you no right to joy, or even to give joy to others?"

"Tell me more about the case that is interesting you. Supposing you found Harriet Smith or her children?"

"I would show them the will and put them in the way of securing their fortune."

"*I* should like to see that will."

"Would you?"

"Yes, it would interest me."

"You do not look very interested."

"Do I not? Yet I am, I assure you."

"Then you shall see it, or rather this newspaper copy of it which I happen to have in my pocket-book."

"What, that little slip?"

"It is not very large."

"I thought a will was something ponderous."

"Sometimes it is, but this is short and very much to the point; it was drawn up in haste."

"Let me take it," said she.

She took it and carried it over to the lamp. Suddenly she turned about and her face was very white.

"What odd provision is this," she cried, "about the heir being required to live a year in the house where this woman died?"

"Oh," said he, "that is nothing; any one who inherits this money would not mind such a condition as that. Mrs. Wakeham wanted the house fitted up, you see. It had been her birthplace."

Hermione silently handed him back the slip. She looked so agitated that he was instantly struck by it.

"Why are you affected by this?" he cried. "Hermione, Hermione, this is something to *you*!"

She roused herself and looked calmly at him, shaking her head.

"You are mistaken," she declared. "It is nothing to me."

"To some one you know, then,—to your sister?"

"How could it be anything to her, if not to me?"

"True; I beg your pardon; but you seem to feel a personal disappointment."

"You do not understand me very well," said she, and turned towards the door in welcome of her sister, who just then came in. She was followed by

Doris with a tray on which were heaped masses of black and white cherries in bountiful profusion.

"From our own trees," said Emma, as she handed him a plate.

He made his acknowledgments, and leaned forward to take the cherries which Doris offered him.

"Sir," whispered that woman, as she pushed into view a little note which she held in her hand under the tray, "just read this, and I won't disobey you again. It's something you ought to know. For the young ladies' sakes do read it, sir."

He was very angry, and cast her a displeased look, but he took the note. Hermione was at the other end of the room, and Emma was leaning over her aunt, so the action was not seen; but he felt guilty of a discourtesy for all that, and ate his cherries with a disturbed mind. Doris, on the contrary, looked triumphant, and passed from one to the other with a very cheerful smile.

When Frank arrived home he read that note. It was from Doris herself, and ran thus:

> "Something has happened to the young ladies. They were to have had new dresses this month, and now they say they must make the old ones do. There is less too for dinner than there was, and if it were not for the fruit on our trees we would not have always enough to eat. But that is not the worst; Miss Emma says I shall have to leave them, as they cannot pay me any longer for my work. As if I would leave them, if I starved! Do, do find out what this means, for it is too much to believe that they are going to be poor with all the rest they have to endure."

Find out what it meant! He knew what it meant; they had sacrificed their case, and now they must go hungry, wear old clothes, and possibly do their own work. It made him heart-sick; it made him desperate; it made him wellnigh forget her look when she said: "Our friendship must not grow into love, *must not*, I say, for both our sakes. It would be fatal."

He resolved to see Hermione the next morning, and, if possible, persuade her to listen to reason, and give up a resolve that endangered both her own and her sister's future comfort.

XIV.
IN THE NIGHT WATCHES.

Meantime in the old house Hermione sat watching Emma as she combed out her long hair before the tiny mirror in their bedroom. Her face, relieved now from all effort at self-control, betrayed a deep discouragement, which deepened its tragic lines and seemed to fill the room with gloom. Yet she said nothing till Emma had finished her task and looked around, then she exclaimed:

"Another curse has fallen upon us; we might have been rich, but must remain poor. Do you think we can bear many more disappointments, Emma?"

"I do not think that I can," murmured Emma, with a pitiful smile. "But what do you mean by riches? Gaining our case would not have made us rich."

"No."

"Has—has Mr. Etheridge offered himself? Have you had a chance of *that* happiness, and refused it?"

Hermione, who had been gazing almost sadly at her sister as she spoke the foregoing words, flushed, half angrily, half disdainfully, and answered with sufficient bitterness in her voice:

"Could I accept any man's devotion *now*! Could I accept even *his* if it were offered to me? Emma, your memory seems very short, or you have never realized the position in which I stand."

Emma, who had crimsoned as painfully as her sister at that one emphasized word, which suggested so much to both sisters, did not answer for a moment, but when she did her words came with startling distinctness.

"You do me wrong; I not only have realized, to the core of my heart, your position and what it demands, but I have shared it, as you know, and never more than when the question came up as to whether we girls could marry with such a shadow hanging over us."

"Emma, what do you mean?" asked Hermione, rising and confronting her sister, with wide open, astonished eyes. For Emma's appearance was startling, and might well thrill an observer who had never before seen her gentleness disturbed by a passion as great as she herself might feel.

But Emma, at the first sight of this reflection of her own emotions in Hermione's face, calmed her manner, and put a check upon her expression.

"If you do not know," said she, "I had rather not be the one to tell you. But never say again that I do not realize your position."

"Emma, Emma," pursued Hermione, without a change of tone or any diminution in the agitation of her manner to show that she had heard these words, "have *you* had a lover and I not know it? Did you give up that *when——*" The elder sister choked; the younger smiled, but with an infinite sadness.

"I should not have spoken of it," said she; "I would not have done so, but that I hoped to influence you to look on this affair with different eyes. I—I believe you ought to embrace this new hope, Hermione. Do but tell him——"

"*Tell him!* that would be a way to gain him surely."

"I do not think it would cause you to lose him; that is, if you could assure him that your heart is free to love him as such a man ought to be loved."

The question in these words made Hermione blush and turn away; but her emotion was nothing to that of the quieter sister, who, after she had made this suggestion, stood watching its effect with eyes in which the pain and despair of a year seemed at once to flash forth to light.

"I honor him," began Hermione, in a low, broken voice, "but you know it was not honor simply that I felt for——"

"Do not speak his name," flashed out Emma. "He—you—do not care for each other, or—or—you and I would never be talking as we are doing here to-night. I am sure you have forgotten him, Hermione, for all your hesitations and efforts to be faithful. I have seen it in your eyes for weeks, I have heard it in your voice when you have spoken to this new friend. Why then deceive yourself; why let a worn-out memory stand in the way of a new joy, a real joy, an unsullied and wholly promising happiness?"

"Emma! Emma, what has come to you? You never talked to me like this before. Is it the memory of this folly only that stands in the way of what you so astonishingly advocate? Can a woman situated as I am, give herself up to any hope, any joy?"

"Yes, for the situation will change when you yield yourself once again to the natural pleasures of life. I do not believe in the attitude you have taken, Hermione; I have never believed in it, yet I have cheerfully shared it because, because—you know why; do not let us talk of those days."

"You do not know all my provocation," quoth Hermione.

"Perhaps not, but nothing can excuse the sacrifice you are making of your life. Consider, Hermione. Why should you? Have you not duties to the present, as well as to the past? Should you not think of the long years that may lie between this hour and a possible old age, years which might be filled with beneficence and love, but which now— —"

"Emma, Emma, what are you saying? Are you so tired of sharing my fate that you would try to make me traitor to my word, traitor to my love— —"

"Hush," whispered again Emma, "you do not love *him*. Answer me, if you do. Plunge deep into your heart, and say if you feel as you did once; I want to hear the words from your lips, but be honest."

"Would it be any credit to me if I did not? Would you think more of me if I acknowledged the past was a mistake, and that I wrecked my life for a passion which a year's absence could annul."

But the tender Emma was inexorable, and held her sister by the hands while she repeated.

"Answer, answer! or I shall take your very refusal for a reply."

But Hermione only drooped her head, and finally drew away her hands.

"You seem to prefer the cause of this new man," she murmured ironically. "Perhaps you think he will make the better brother-in-law."

The flush on Emma's cheek spread till it dyed her whole neck.

"I think," she observed gravely, "that Mr. Etheridge is the more devoted to you, Hermione. Dr. Sellick—" what did not that name cost her?—"has not even looked up at our windows when riding by the house."

Hermione's eye flashed, and she bounded imperiously to her feet.

"And that is why I think that he still remembers. And shall I forget?" she murmured more softly, "while he cherishes one thought of grief or chagrin over the past?"

Emma, whose head had fallen on her breast, played idly with her long hair, and softly drew it across her face.

"If you knew," she murmured, "that he did not cherish one thought such as you imagine, would you then open your heart to this new love and the brightness in the world and all the hopes which belong to our time of life."

"If, if," repeated Hermione, staring at the half-hidden face of her sister as at some stranger whom she had found persistent and incomprehensible. "I don't know what you mean by your *ifs*. Do you think it would add to my content and self-satisfaction to hear that I had reared this ghastly prison which I inhabit on a foundation of sand, and that the walls in toppling would crash about my ears and destroy me? You must have a strange idea of a woman's heart, if you thought it would make me any readier to face life if I knew I had sacrificed my all to a chimera."

Emma sighed. "Not if it gave you a new hope," she whispered.

"Ah," murmured Hermione, and her face softened for the first time. "I dare not think of that," she murmured. "I dare not, Emma;I dare not."

The younger sister, as if answered, threw back her hair and looked at Hermione quite brightly.

"You will come to dare in time," said she, and fled from the room like a spirit.

When she was gone, Hermione stood still for many minutes; then she began quietly to let down her own hair. As the long locks fell curling and dark about her shoulders, a dreamier and dreamier spirit came upon her, mellowing the light in her half-closed eyes, and bringing such a sweet, half-timid, half-longing smile to her lips that she looked the embodiment of virginal joy. But the mood did not last long, and ere the thick curls were duly parted and arranged for the night, the tears had begun to fall, and the sobs to come till she was fain to put out her light and hide behind the curtains of her bed the grief and remorse which were pressing upon her.

Meanwhile Emma had stolen to her aunt's room, and was kneeling down beside her peaceful figure.

"Aunt, dear Aunt," she cried, "tell me what my duty is. Help me to decide if Hermione should be told the truth which we have so long kept from her."

She knew the old lady could not hear, but she was in the habit of speaking to her just as if she could, and often through some subtle sympathy between them the sense of her words was understood and answered in a way to surprise her.

And in this case Mrs. Lovell seemed to understand, for she kissed Emma with great fondness, and then, taking the sweet, troubled, passionate face between her two palms, looked at her with such love and sympathy that the tears filled Emma's eyes, for all her efforts at self-control.

"Tell her," came forth at last, in the strange, loud tones of the perfectly deaf, "and leave the rest to God. You have kept silence, and the wound has not healed; now try the truth, and may heaven bless you and the two others whom you desire to make happy."

And Emma, rising up, thanked God that he had left them this one blessing in their desolation—this true-hearted and tender-souled adviser.

That night, as Hermione was tossing in a restless sleep, she suddenly became aware of a touch on her shoulder, and, looking up, she saw her sister standing before her, with a lighted candle in her hand, and her hair streaming about her.

"What is the matter?" she cried, bounding up in terror, for Emma's face was livid with its fixed resolve, and wore a look such as Hermione had never seen there before.

"Nothing," cried the other, "nothing; only I have something to tell you—something which you should have known a long time ago—something about which you should never have been deceived. It is this, Hermione. It was not you Dr. Sellick wished to marry, but myself." And with the words the light was blown out, and Hermione found herself alone.

BOOK II.
THE SECRET OF THE LABORATORY.

XV.
THE BEGINNING OF CHANGES.

As Frank went by the house early the next morning on his way to the train, he paused and glanced at one of the upper windows, where he had once before seen Hermione's face looking out. The blinds were closed, but the slats were slightly turned, and through them he thought, but he could not be quite sure, he caught the glimpse of a pair of flashing eyes. In the hope that this was so, he laid his hand upon the gate and then glanced up again, as if asking permission to open it. The blinds moved and in another instant fell back, and he saw the face he loved, looking very pale but sweet, bending towards him from the clustering honeysuckles.

"May I come in," he asked, "just for a few words more? You know we were interrupted last night."

She shook her head, and his heart sank; then she seemed to repent her decision and half opened her lips as if to speak, but no words came. He kept his hand on the gate, and his face grew eloquent.

"You cannot say no," he now pleaded, smiling at the blush that was slowly mantling on her cheek. "I may not be here again for weeks, and if you do not let me say good-by I shall always think I have displeased you, and that will not add to my happiness or peace."

"Wait," came in sudden eagerness from her lips, and he saw her disappear from the window and appear, almost before he could realize his own relief, in the open door-way before him. "Come in," said she, with the first full glad smile he had ever seen on her lips.

But though he bounded up the steps he did not enter the house. Instead of that he seized her hand and tried to induce her to come out in the open air to him. "No close rooms," said he, "on such a morning as this. Come into the poplar-walk, come; let me see you with the wind blowing your hair about your cheeks."

"No, no!" burst from her lips in something almost like fright. "Emma goes into the garden, but not I. Do not ask me to break the habit of months, do not."

But he was determined, tenderly, firmly determined.

"I must," said he; "I must. Your white cheeks and worn face demand the freshness of out-door air. I do not say you must go outside the gate, but I do say you must feel again what it is to have the poplars rustle above your head and the grass close lovingly over your feet. So come, Hermione, come, for I will not take no, I will not, even from the lips whose business it shall be to command me in everything else."

His eyes entreated her, his hand constrained her; she sought to do battle with his will, but her glances fell before the burning ardor of his. With a sudden wild heave of her breast, she yielded, and he drew her down into the garden and so around to the poplar-walk. As she went the roses came out on her cheeks, and she seemed to breathe like a creature restored to life.

"Oh, the blue, blue sky!" she cried, "and oh, the hills! I have not seen them for a year. As for the poplars, I should love to kiss their old boughs, I am so glad to be beneath them once more."

But as she proceeded farther her spirits seemed to droop again, and she cast him furtive looks as much as to say:

"Is it right? ought I to be enjoying all this bliss?"

But the smile on his face was so assured, she speedily took courage again, and allowed him to lead her to the end of the poplar-walk, far up in those regions where his eye had often strayed but his feet never been even in fancy. On a certain bench they sat down, and he turned towards her a beaming face.

"Now I feel as if you were mine," he cried. "Nothing shall part us after this, not even your own words."

But she put her hands out with a meek, deprecating gesture, very unlike the imperious one she had indulged in before.

"You must not say that," she cried. "My coming out may have been a weakness, but it shall not be followed by what you yourself might come to regard as a wrong. I am here, and it was for your pleasure I came, but that commits me to nothing and you to nothing, unless it be to the momentary delight. Do you hear that bird sing?"

"You are lovely with that flickering sunlight on your face," was all the reply he made.

And perhaps he could have made no better, for it gave her a sweet sense of helplessness in the presence of this great love, which to a woman who had been so long bearing herself up in solitary assertion had all the effect of rest and relief.

"You make me feel as if my youth was not quite gone," said she; "but," she added, as his hand stole towards hers, "you have not yet made me feel that I must listen to all the promptings of love. There is a gulf between me and you across which we cannot shake hands. But we can speak, friend, to one another, and that is a pleasure to one who has travelled so long in a wilderness alone. Shall we not let that content us, or do you wish to risk life and all by attempting more?"

"I wish to risk everything, anything, so as to make you mine."

"You do not know what you are saying. We are talking pure foolishness," was her sudden exclamation, as she leapt to her feet. "Here, in this pure air, and in sight of the fields and hills, the narrow, confining bands which have held me to the house seem to lose their power and partake of the unsubstantiality of a dream. But I know that with my recrossing of the threshold they will resume their power again, and I shall wonder I could ever talk of freedom or companionship with one who does not know the secrets of the house or the shadow which has been cast by them upon my life."

"You know them, and yet you would go back," he cried. "I should say the wiser course would be to turn away from a place so fatal to your happiness and hopes, and, yielding to my entreaties, go with me to the city, where we will be married, and——"

"Frank, what a love you have for me! a love which questions nothing, not even my past, notwithstanding I say it is that past which separates us and makes me the recluse I am."

"You have filled me with trust by the pure look in your eyes," said he. "Why should I ask you to harrow up your feelings by telling me what you would have told me long ago, if it had not been too painful?"

"You are a great, good man," she cried. "You subdue me who have never been subdued before, except by my own passionate temper. I reverence you and I—love—you. Do not ask me to say anything more." And the queenly, imperious form swayed from side to side, and the wild tears gushed forth, and she fled from his side down the poplar-walk, till she came within sight of the house, when she paused, gathering up her strength till he reached the place where she stood, when she said:

"You are coming again, some time?"

"I am coming again in a week."

"You will find a little packet awaiting you in the place where you stay. You will read it before you see me again?"

"I will read it."

"Good-by," said she; and her face in its most beautiful aspect shone on him for a moment; then she retreated, and was lost to his view in the shrubbery.

As he passed the house on his way to the gate, he saw Doris casting looks of delight down the poplar-walk, where her young mistress was still straying, and at the same instant caught a hurried glimpse of Mrs. Lovell and Emma, leaning from the window above, in joyful recognition of the fact that a settled habit had been broken, and that at his inducement Hermione had consented to taste again the out-door air.

He was yet in time for the train, for he had calculated on this visit, and so made allowances for it. He was therefore on the point of turning towards the station, when he saw the figure of a man coming down the street, and stopped, amazed. Was it—could it be—yes, it was Hiram Huckins. He was dressed in black, and looked decent, almost trim, but his air was that of one uncertain of himself, and his face was disfigured by an ingratiating leer which Etheridge found almost intolerable. He was the first to speak.

"How do you do, Mr. Etheridge?" said he, ambling up, and bowing with hypocritical meekness. "You didn't expect to see me here, did you? But business calls me. My poor, dear sister Harriet is said to have been in Marston, and I have come to see if it is true. I do not find her, do you?"

The sly, half-audacious, half-deprecating look with which he uttered these words irritated Frank beyond endurance.

"No," he rejoined. "Your valuable time will be wasted here. You will have to look elsewhere for your *dear* sister."

"It has taken you a long time to find that out," insinuated the other, with his most disagreeable leer. "I suppose, now, you thought till this very last night that you would find her in the graveyard or in some of these old houses. Else why should you waste *your* valuable time in a place of such mean attractions."

They were standing directly in front of the Cavanagh house and Frank was angry enough to lift his hand against him at these words, for the old man's eyes—he was not old but he always presented the appearance of being so—had wandered meaningly towards the windows above him, as if he knew that behind them, instead of in any graveyard, centred the real attractions of the place for Frank.

But though a lawyer may have passions, he, as a rule, has learned to keep a curb upon them, especially in the presence of one who is likely to oppose him.

So bowing with an effort at politeness, young Etheridge acknowledged that he had only lately given up his hope, and was about to withdraw in his haste to catch the train, when Huckins seized him by the arm with a low chuckle and slyly whispered:

"You've been visiting the two pretty hermitesses, eh? Are they nice girls? Do they know anything about my sister? You look as if you had heard good news somewhere. Was it in there?"

He was eager; he was insinuating; he seemed to hang upon Frank's reply. But the lawyer, struck and troubled by this allusion to the women he so cherished, on lips he detested beyond any in the world, stood still for a moment, looking the indignation he dared not speak.

Huckins took advantage of this silence to speak again, this time with an off-hand assurance only less offensive than his significant remarks.

"I know they keep at home and do not go out in the world to hear the gossip. But women who keep themselves shut up often know a lot about what is going on around them, Mr. Etheridge, and as you have been there I thought—"

"Never mind what you thought," burst out Frank, unable to bear his insinuations any longer. "Enough that I do not go there to hear anything about Harriet Smith. There are other law cases in the world besides yours, and other clients besides your sister and her heirs. These young ladies, for instance, whom you speak of so freely."

"I am sure," stammered Huckins, with great volubility, and an air of joviality which became him as little as the suspicious attitude he had hitherto taken, "I never meant to speak with the least disrespect of ladies I have never met. Only I was interested you know, naturally interested, in anything which might seem to bear upon my own affairs. They drag so, don't they, Mr. Etheridge, and I am kept so long out of my rights."

"No longer than justice seems to demand, Mr. Huckins; your sister, and her heirs, if they exist, have rights also."

"So you say," quoth Huckins, "and I have learned not to quarrel with a lawyer. Good-day, Mr. Etheridge, good-day. Hope to hear that some decision has been arrived at soon."

"Good-day," growled Frank, and strode rapidly off, determined to return to Marston that very night if only to learn what Huckins was up to. But before he had gone a dozen steps he came quickly back and seized that person by the arm. "Where are you going?" he asked; for Huckins had laid his hand on Miss Cavanagh's gate and was about to enter.

"I am going to pay a visit," was the smiling reply. "Is there anything wrong in that?"

"I thought you did not know these young ladies—that they were strangers to you?"

"So they are, so they are, but I am a man who takes a great interest in eccentric persons. I am eccentric myself; so was my sister Cynthia; so I may say was Harriet, though how eccentric we have still to find out. If the young ladies do not want to see an old man from New York they can say so, but I mean to give them the chance. Have you anything to say against it?"

"No, except that I think it an unwarrantable intrusion about which you had better think twice."

"I have thought," retorted Huckins, with a mild obstinacy that had a sinister element in it, "and I can't deny myself the pleasure. Think of it! two healthy and beautiful girls under twenty-four who never leave the house they live in! That is being more unlike folks than Cynthia and myself, who were old and who had a fortune to guard. Besides we did leave the house, or rather I did, when there was business to look after or food to buy. But they don't go out for anything, I hear, *anything*. Mr. Ruthven—he is the minister you know—has given me his card by way of introduction; so you see they will have to treat me politely, and that means I shall at least see their faces."

His cunning, his satisfaction, and a certain triumph underlying all, affected Frank like the hiss of a serpent. But the business awaiting him in New York was imperative, and the time remaining to him before the train left was barely enough to enable him to reach the station. So curbing his disgust and the dread he had of seeing this knave enter Hermione's door, he tore himself away and made what haste he could to the station. He arrived just as the first whistle of the coming train was heard, and owing to a short delay occasioned by the arrival of a telegram at the station, he was enabled to write two notes, one to Miss Cavanagh and one to Dr. Sellick. These he delivered to Jerry, with strict injunctions to deliver them immediately, and as the train moved off carrying him back to his duties, he had the satisfaction of seeing the lumbering figure of that slow but reliable messenger disappear around the curve in the highway which led directly to Miss Cavanagh's house.

XVI.
A STRANGE VISITOR.

Frank's visit and interview with Hermione had this advantage for the latter, that it took away some of the embarrassment which her first meeting with Emma, after the revelations of the night before, had necessarily occasioned. She had breakfasted in her own room, feeling that it would be impossible for her to meet her sister's eye, but having been led into giving such proof of her preference for Mr. Etheridge, and the extent of his influence over her, there could of course be no further question of Dr. Sellick, or any need for explanations between herself and Emma regarding a past thus shown to be no longer of vital interest to her. When, therefore, she came in from the garden and saw Emma waiting for her at the side-door, she blushed, but that was all, in memory of the past night; and murmuring some petty commonplace, sought to pass her and enter again the house which she had not left before in a full year.

But Emma, who was bright with a hope she had not felt in months, stopped her with a word.

"There is an old man waiting in the parlor who says he wants to see us. He sent in this card—it has Dr. Ruthven's name on it—and Doris says he seemed very eager and anxious. Can you guess who he can be?"

"No," rejoined Hermione, wondering. "But we can soon see. Our visitors are not so numerous that we can afford to slight one." And tripping by Emma, she led the way into the parlor.

A slight, meagre, eager-eyed man, clad in black and wearing a propitiatory smile on very thin lips, rose as she entered, and bowed with an awkward politeness that yet had something of the breeding of a gentleman in it.

Hermione did not like his looks, but she advanced cordially enough, perhaps because her heart was lighter than usual, and her mind less under the strain of one horrible fixed idea than it had been in months.

"How do you do?" said she, and looked at him inquiringly.

Huckins, with another bow, this time in recognition of her unexpected beauty and grace, shambled uneasily forward, and said in a hard, strained voice which was even more disagreeable than his face:

"I am sure you are very good to receive me, Miss Cavanagh. I—I had a great desire to come. Your father——"

She drew back with a gasp.

"My father——" she repeated.

"Was an old friend of mine," he went on, in a wheedling tone, in seeming oblivion of the effect his words had had upon her. "Did you never hear him speak of Hope, Seth Hope?"

"Never," cried Hermione, panting, and looking appealingly at Emma, who had just entered the room.

"Yet we were friends for years," declared the dissimulator, folding his hands with a dreary shake of his head.

"For years?" repeated Emma, advancing and surveying him earnestly.

"Our father was a much older man than you, Mr.—Mr. Hope."

"Perhaps, perhaps, I never saw him. But we corresponded for years. Have you not come across letters signed by my name, in looking over his effects?"

"No," answered Emma, firmly, while Hermione, looking very pale, retreated towards the door, where she stopped in mingled distress and curiosity.

"Then he must have destroyed them all," declared their visitor. "Some people do not keep letters. Yet they were full of information, I assure you; full, for it was upon the ever delightful subject of chemistry we corresponded, and the letters I wrote him sometimes cost me a week's effort to indite."

Emma, who had never met a man like this before, looked at him with wide-open eyes. Had Hermione not been there, she would have liked to have played with his eccentricities, and asked him numberless questions. But with her sister shrinking in the doorway, she dared not encourage him to pursue a theme which she perceived to be fraught with the keenest suffering for Hermione. So she refrained from showing the distrust which she really felt, and motioning the old man to sit down, asked, quietly:

"And was it for these letters you came? If so, I am sorry that none such have been found."

"No, no," cried Huckins, with stammering eagerness, as he marked the elder sister's suspicious eyes and unencouraging manner. "It was not to get them back that I ventured to call upon you, but for the pleasure of seeing the house where he lived and did so much wonderful work, and the laboratory, if you will be so good. Why has your sister departed?" he suddenly inquired, in fretful surprise, pointing to the door where Hermione had stood a moment before.

"She probably has duties," observed Emma, in a troubled voice. "And she probably was surprised to hear a stranger ask to see a room no one but the members of his family have entered since our father's death."

"But I am not a stranger," artfully pursued the cringing Huckins, making himself look as benevolent as he could. "I am an admirer, a devoted admirer of your remarkable parent, and I could show you papers" — but he never did, — "of writing in that same parent's hand, in which he describes the long, narrow room, with its shelves full of retorts and crucibles, and the table where he used to work, with the mystic signs above it, which some said were characters taken from cabalistic books, but which he informed me were the new signs he wished to introduce into chemistry, as being more comprehensive and less liable to misinterpretation than those now in use."

"You do seem to know something about the room," she murmured softly, too innocent to realize that the knowledge he showed was such as he could have gleaned from any of Mr. Cavanagh's intimate friends.

"But I want to see it with my own eyes. I want to stand in the spot where he stood, and drink in the inspiration of his surroundings, before I go back to my own great labor."

"Have you a laboratory? Are you a chemist?" asked Emma, interested in despite of the dislike his wheedling ways and hypocritical air naturally induced.

"Yes, yes, I have a laboratory," said he; "but there is no romance about mine; it is just the plain working-room of a hard-working man, while his— —"

Emma, who had paled at these words almost as much as her sister had done at his first speech about her father, recoiled with a look in which the wonderment was strangely like fear.

"I cannot show you the room," said she. "You exaggerate your desire to see it, as you exaggerate the attainments and the discoveries of my father. I must ask you to excuse me," she continued, with a slight acknowledgment in which dismissal could be plainly read. "I am very busy, and the morning is rapidly flying. If you could come again— —"

But here Hermione's full deep tones broke from the open doorway.

"If he wishes to see the place where father worked, let him come; there is no reason why we should hide it from one who professes such sympathy with our father's pursuits."

Huckins, chuckling, looked at Emma, and then at her sister, and moved rapidly towards the door. Emma, who had been taken greatly by surprise by her sister's words, followed slowly, showing more and more astonishment as Hermione spoke of this place, or that, on their way up-stairs, as being the spot where her father's books were kept, or his chemicals stored, till they came to the little twisted staircase at the top, when she became suddenly silent.

It was now Emma's turn to say:

"This is the entrance to the laboratory. You see it is just as you have described it."

Huckins, with a sly leer, stepped into the room, and threw around one quick, furtive look which seemed to take in the whole place in an instant. It was similar to his description, and yet it probably struck him as being very different from the picture he had formed of it in his imagination. Long, narrow, illy lighted, and dreary, it offered anything but a cheerful appearance, even in the bright July sunshine that sifted through the three small windows ranged along its side. At one end was a row of shelves extending from the floor to the ceiling, filled with jars, chemicals, and apparatus of various kinds. At the other end was a table for collecting gases, and beneath each window were more shelves, and more chemicals, and more apparatus. A large electric machine perched by itself in one corner, gave a grotesque air to that part of the room, but the chief impression made upon an observer was one of bareness and desolation, as of the husk of something which had departed, leaving a smell of death behind. The girls used the room for their dreary midnight walks; otherwise it was never entered, except by Doris, who kept it in perfect order, as a penance, she was once heard to declare, she having a profound dislike to the place, and associating it always, as we have before intimated, with some tragic occurrence which she believed to have taken place there.

Huckins, after his first quick look, chuckled and rubbed his hands together, in well-simulated glee.

"Do I see it?" he cried; "*the room* where the great Cavanagh thought and worked! It is a privilege not easily over-estimated." And he flitted from shelf to drawer, from drawer to table, with gusts of enthusiasm which made the cold, stern face of Hermione, who had taken up her stand in the doorway, harden into an expression of strange defiance.

Emma, less filled with some dark memory, or more swayed by her anxiety to fathom his purposes, and read the secret of an intrusion which as yet was nothing but a troublous mystery to her, had entered the room with him, and stood quietly watching his erratic movements, as if she half expected him to abstract something from the hoard of old chemicals or collection of formulas above which he hung with such a pretence of rapture.

"How good! how fine! how interesting!" broke in shrill ejaculation from his lips as he ambled hither and thither. But Emma noticed that his eye ever failed to dwell upon what was really choice or unique in the collection of her father's apparatus, and that when by chance he touched an alembic or lifted a jar, it was with an awkwardness that betrayed an unaccustomed hand.

"You do not hold a retort in that way," she finally remarked, going up to him and taking the article in question out of his hand. "This is how my father was accustomed to handle them," she proceeded, and he, taken aback for the instant, blushed and murmured something about her father being his superior and she the very apt pupil of a great scholar and a very wise man.

"You wanted to see the laboratory, and now you have seen it," quoth Hermione from her place by the door. "Is there anything else we can do for you?"

The chill, stern tones seemed to rouse him and he turned towards the speaker.

"No, no, my dear, no, no. You have been very good." But Emma noticed that his eyes still kept roaming here, there, and everywhere while he spoke, picking up information as a bird picks up worms.

"What does he want?" thought she, looking anxiously towards her sister.

"You have a very pleasant home," he now remarked, pausing at the head of those narrow stairs and peering into the nest of Hermione's own room, the door of which stood invitingly open. "Is that why you never leave it?" he unexpectedly asked, looking with his foxy eyes from one sister to the other.

"I do not think it is necessary for us to answer you," said Emma, while Hermione, with a flash in her eye, motioned him imperiously down, saying as she slowly followed him:

"Our friends do not consider it wise to touch upon that topic, how much more should a stranger hesitate before doing so?"

And he, cowering beneath her commanding look and angry presence, seemed to think she was right in this and ventured no more, though his restless eyes were never still, and he appeared to count the very banisters as his hand slid down the railing, and to take in every worn thread that showed itself in the carpet over which his feet shuffled in almost undignified haste.

When they were all below, he made one final remark:

"Your father owed me money, but I do not think of pressing my claim. You do not look as if you were in a position to satisfy it."

"Ah," exclaimed Emma, thinking she had discovered the motive of his visit at last; "that is why you wanted to see the laboratory."

"Partly," he acknowledged with a sly wink, "but not altogether. All there is there would not buy up the I. O. U. I hold. I shall have to let the matter go with other bad debts I suppose. But three hundred dollars is a goodly sum, young ladies, a goodly sum."

Emma, who knew that her father had not been above borrowing money for his experiments, looked greatly distressed for a moment, but Hermione, who had now taken her usual place as leader, said without attempting to disguise the tone of suspicion in her voice:

"Substantiate your claim and present your bill and we will try to pay it. We have still a few articles of furniture left."

Huckins, who had never looked more hypocritically insinuating or more diabolically alert, exclaimed,

"I can wait, I can wait."

But Hermione, with a grand air and a candid look, answered bitterly and at once:

"What we cannot do now we can never do. Our fortunes are not likely to increase in the future, so you had better put in your claim at once, if you really want your pay."

"You think so?" he began; and his eye, which had been bright before, now gleamed with the excitement of a fear allayed. "I——"

But just then the bell rang with a loud twang, and he desisted from finishing his sentence.

Emma went to the door and soon came back with a letter which she handed to Hermione.

"The man Jerry brought it," she explained, casting a meaning look at her sister.

Hermione, with a quick flush, stepped to the window and in the shadow of the curtains read her note. It was a simple word of warning.

Dear Miss Cavanagh:

I met a man at your gate who threatened to go in. Do not receive him, or if you have already done so, distrust every word he has uttered and cut the interview short. He is Hiram Huckins, the man concerning whom I spoke so frankly when we were discussing the will of the Widow Wakeham.

Yours most truly,

Frank Etheridge.

The flush with which Hermione read these lines was quite gone when she turned to survey the intruder, who had forced himself upon her confidence and that of her sister by means of a false name. Indeed she looked strangely pale and strangely indignant as she met his twinkling and restless eye, and, to any one who knew the contents of the note which she held, it would seem that her first words must be those of angry dismissal.

But instead of these, she first looked at him with some curiosity, and then said in even, low, and slightly contemptuous tones:

"Will you not remain and lunch with us, Mr. Huckins?"

At this unexpected utterance of his name he gave a quick start, but soon was his cringing self again. Glancing at the letter she held, he remarked:

"My dear young lady, I see that Mr. Etheridge has been writing to you. Well, there is no harm in that. Now we can shake hands in earnest"; and as he held out his wicked, trembling palm, his face was a study for a painter.

XVII.
TWO CONVERSATIONS.

That afternoon, as Emma was sitting in her own room, she was startled by the unexpected presence of Hermione. As they were not in the habit of intruding upon each other above stairs, Emma rose in some surprise. But Hermione motioning her back into her chair, fell at her feet in sudden abandon, and, laying her head in her sister's lay, gave way to one deep sob. Emma, too much astonished to move at this unexpected humiliation of one who had never before bent her imperious head in that household, looked at the rich black locks scattered over her knees with wonder if not with awe.

"Hermione!" she whispered, "Hermione! do not kneel to me, unless it be with joy."

But the elder sister, clasping her convulsively around the waist, murmured:

"Let me be humble for a moment; let me show that I have something in me besides pride, reckless endurance, and determined will. I have not shown it enough in the past. I have kept my sufferings to myself, and my remorse to myself, and alas! also all my stern recognition of your love and unparalleled devotion. I have felt your goodness, oh, I have felt it, so much so, at times, that I thought I could not live, ought not to live, just because of what I have done to *you*; but I never said anything, could not say anything! Yet all the remorse I experienced was nothing to what I experience now that I know I was not even loved— —"

"Hush," broke in Emma, "let those days be forgotten. I only felt that you ought to know the truth, because sweeter prospects are before you, and— —"

"I understand," murmured Hermione, "you are always the great-hearted, unselfishly minded sister. I believe you would actually rejoice to see me happy now, even if it did not release you from the position you have assumed. But it shall release you; you shall not suffer any longer on my account. Even if it is only to give you the opportunity of—of meeting with Dr. Sellick, you shall go out of this house to-day. Do you hear me, Emma, *to-day*?"

But the ever-gentle, ever-docile Emma rose up at this, quite pale in her resolution. "Till you put foot out of the gate I remain this side of it," said she. "Nothing can ever alter my determination in this regard."

And Hermione, surveying her with slowly filling eyes, became convinced that it would be useless to argue this point, though she made an effort to do so by saying with a noble disregard of her own womanly shame which in its turn caused Emma's eyes to fill:

"Dr. Sellick has suffered a great wrong, I judge; don't you think you owe something to him?"

But Emma shook her head, though she could not prevent a certain wistful look from creeping into her face. "Not what I owe to you," said she, and then flushed with distress lest her sister should misjudge the meaning of her words.

But Hermione was in a rarely generous mood. "But I release you from any promise you have made or any obligations you may consider yourself to be under. Great heaven! do you think I would hold you to them *now?*"

"I hold myself," cried Emma. "You cannot release me,—except," she added, with gentle intimation, "by releasing yourself."

"I cannot release myself," moaned Hermione. "If we all perish I cannot release myself. *I* am a prisoner to this house, but you——"

"We are sister prisoners," interpolated Emma, softly. Then with a sudden smile, "I was in hopes that he who led you to break one resolution might induce you to break another."

But Hermione, flushing with something of her old fire, cried out warmly: "In going out of the house I broke a promise made to myself, but in leaving the grounds I should—oh, I cannot tell you what I should do; not even you know the full bitterness of my life! It is a secret, locked in this shrinking, tortured heart, which it almost breaks, but does not quite, or I should not linger in this dreadful world to be a cause of woe to those I cherish most."

"But Hermione, Hermione——"

"You think you know what has set a seal on my lips, the gloom on my brow, the death in my heart; but you do not, Emma. You know much, but not the fatal grief, the irrepressible misery. But you shall know, and know soon. I have promised to write out the whole history of my life for Mr. Etheridge, and when he has read it you shall read it too. Perhaps when you learn what the real horror of this house has been, you may appreciate the force of will-power which it has taken for me to remain in it."

Emma, who had never suspected anything in the past beyond what she herself knew, grew white with fresh dismay. But Hermione, seeing it, kissed her, and, speaking more lightly, said: "You kept back one vital secret from me in consideration of what you thought the limit of my endurance. I have done the same for you under the same consideration. Now we will equalize matters, and perhaps—who knows?—happier days may come, if Mr. Etheridge is not too much startled by the revelations I have to make him, and if Dr. Sellick— do not shrink, Emma—learns some magnanimity from his friend and will accept the explanations I shall think it my duty to offer him."

But at this suggestion, so unlike any that had ever come from Hermione's lips before, the younger sister first stared, and then flung her arms around the speaker, with cries of soft deprecation and shame.

"You shall not," she murmured. "Not if I lose him shall he ever know why that cruel letter was written. It is enough—it shall be enough—that he was dismissed *then*. If he loves me he will try his fate again. But I do not think he does love me, and it would be better for him that he did not. Would *he* ever marry a woman who, not even at his entreaty, could be induced to cross the limits of her home?"

"Mr. Etheridge should not do it either; but he is so generous—perhaps so hopeful! He may not be as much so when he has read what I have to write."

"I think he will," said Emma, and then paused, remembering that she did not know all that her sister had to relate.

"He would be a man in a thousand then," whispered the once haughty Hermione. "A man to worship, to sacrifice all and everything to, that it was in one's power to sacrifice."

"He will do what is right," quoth Emma.

Hermione sighed. Was she afraid of the right?

Meantime, in the poplar-walk below, another talk was being held, which, if these young girls could have heard it, might have made them feel even more bitterly than before, what heavy clouds lay upon any prospect of joy which they might secretly cherish. Doris, who was a woman of many thoughts, and who just now found full scope for all her ideas in the unhappy position of her two dear young ladies, had gone into the open air to pick currants and commune with herself as to what more could be done to bring them into a proper recognition of their folly in clinging to a habit or determination which seemed likely to plunge them into such difficulties.

The currant bushes were at the farther end of the garden near the termination of the poplar-walk, and when, in one of the pauses of her picking, she chanced to look up, she saw advancing towards her down that walk the thin, wiry figure of the old man who had taken luncheon with the young ladies, and whom they called, in very peculiar tones, she thought, Mr. Huckins. He was looking from right to left as he came, and his air was one of contemplation or that of a person who was taking in the beauties of a scene new to him and not wholly unpleasant.

When he reached the spot where Doris stood eying him with some curiosity and not a little distrust, he paused, looked about him, and perceiving her, affected some surprise, and stepped briskly to where she was.

"Picking currants?" he observed. "Let me help you. I used to do such things when a boy."

Astonished, and not a little gratified at what she chose to consider his condescension, Doris smiled. It was a rare thing now for a man to be seen in this lonesome old place, and such companionship was not altogether disagreeable to Mistress Doris.

Huckins rubbed his hands together in satisfaction at this smile, and sidled up to the simpering spinster with a very propitiatory air.

"How nice this all is," he remarked. "So rural, so peaceful, and so pleasant. I come from a place where there is no fruit, nor flowers, nor young ladies. You must be happy here." And he gave her a look which she thought very insinuating.

"Oh, I am happy enough," she conceded, "because I am bound to be happy wherever the young ladies are. But I could wish that things were different too." And she thought herself very discreet that she had not spoken more clearly.

"Things?" he repeated softly.

"Yes, my young ladies have odd ideas; I thought you knew."

He drew nearer to her side, very much nearer, and dropped the currants he had plucked gently into her pail.

"I know they have a fixed antipathy to going out, but they will get over that."

"Do you think so?" she asked eagerly.

"Don't *you*?" he queried, with an innocent look of surprise. He was improving in his dissimulation, or else he succeeded better with those of whom he had no fear.

"I don't know what to think. Are you an old friend of theirs?" she inquired. "You must be, to lunch with them."

"I never saw them before to-day," he returned, "yet I am an old friend. Reason that out," he leered.

"You like to puzzle folks," she observed, picking very busily but smiling all the while. "Do you give answers with your puzzles?"

"Not to such sharp wits as yours. But how beautiful Miss Cavanagh is. Has she always had that scar?"

"Ever since I knew her."

"Pity she should have such a blemish. You like her, don't you, very much?"

"I love her."

"And her sister—such a sweet girl!"

"I love them both."

"That is right. I should be sorry to have any one about them who did not love them. *I* love them, or soon shall, very much."

"Are you," Doris inquired, with great inquisitiveness, "going to remain in Marston any time?"

"I cannot say," sighed the old man; "I should like to. I should be very happy here, but I am afraid the young ladies do not like me well enough."

Doris had cherished some such idea herself an hour ago, and had not wondered at it then, but now her feelings seemed changed.

"Was it to see them you came to Marston?" said she.

"Merely to see them," he replied.

She was puzzled, but more eager than puzzled, so anxious was she to find some one who could control their eccentricities.

"They will treat you politely," she assured him. "They are peculiar girls, but they are always polite."

"I am afraid I shall not be satisfied with politeness," he insinuated. "I want them to love me, to confide in me. I want to be their friend in fact as I have so long been in fancy."

"You are some relative of theirs," she now asserted, "or you knew their father well or their mother."

"I wouldn't say no," he replied,—but to which of these three intimations, he evidently did not think it worth while to say.

"Then," she declared, "you are the man I want. Mr. Etheridge—that is the lawyer from New York who has lately been coming here—does not seem to have much confidence in himself or me. But you look as if you might do something or suggest something. I mean about getting the young ladies to give up their whims."

"Has this Mr.—Mr. Etheridge, did you call him?—been doing their business long?"

"I never saw him here till a month ago."

"Ah! a month ago! And do they like him? Do they seem inclined to take his advice? Does he press it upon them?"

"I wish I knew. I am only a poor servant, remember, though my bringing up was as good almost as theirs. They are kind to me, but I do not sit down in the parlor; if I did, I might know something of what is going on. I can only judge, you see, by looks."

"And the looks? Come, I have a *great* interest in the young ladies—almost as great as yours. What do their looks say?—I mean since this young man came to visit them? He is a young man, didn't you say?"

"Yes, he is young, and so good-looking. I have thought—now don't spill the currants, just as we have filled the pail—that he was a little sweet on Miss Hermione, and that that was why he came here so often, and not because he had business."

"You have?" twitted the old man, almost dancing about her in his sudden excitement. "Well, well, that must be seen to. A wedding, eh, a wedding? That's what you think is coming?" And Doris could not tell whether it was pleasure or alarm that gave so queer a look to his eyes.

"I cannot say—I wish I could," she fervently cried; "then I might hope to see a change here; then we might expect to see these two sweet young ladies doing like other folks and making life pleasant for themselves and every one about them. But Miss Hermione is a girl who would be very capable of saying no to a young man if he stood in the way of any resolve she had taken. I don't calculate much on her being influenced by love, or I would never have bothered you with my troubles. It is fear that must control her, or——" Doris paused and looked at him knowingly—"or she must be lured out of the house by some cunning device."

Huckins, who had been feeling his way up to this point, brightened as he noticed the slyness of the smile with which she emphasized this insinuation, and from this moment felt more assured. But he said nothing as yet to show how he was affected by her words. There was another little matter he wanted settled first.

"Do you know," he asked, "why she, and her sister, too, I believe, have taken this peculiar freak? Have they ever told you, or have you ever—" how close his head got to hers, and how he nodded and peered—"surprised their secret?"

Doris shook her head. "All a mystery," she whispered, and began picking currants again, that operation having stopped as they got more earnest.

"But it isn't a mystery," he laughed, "why you want to get them out of the house just *now*. I know your reason for that, and think you will succeed without any device of love or cunning."

"I don't understand you," she protested, puckering her black brows and growing very energetic. "I don't want to do it *now* any more than I have for the last twelve months. Only I am getting desperate. I am not one who can want a thing and be patient. I *want* Miss Hermione Cavanagh and her sister to laugh and be gay like other girls, and till they give up all this nonsense of self-seclusion they never will; and so I say to myself that any measures are justifiable that lead to that end. Don't you think I am right?"

He smiled warily and took her pail of currants from her hand.

"I think you are the brightest woman and have one of the clearest heads I ever knew. I don't remember when I have seen a woman who pleased me so well. Shall we be friends? I am only a solitary bachelor, travelling hither and thither because I do not know how else to spend my money; but I am willing to work for your ends if you are willing to work for mine."

"And what are they?" she simpered, looking very much delighted. Doris was not without ambition, and from this moment not without her hopes.

"To make these young ladies trust me so that I may visit them off and on while I remain in this place. I thought it was pleasant here before, but *now*— —" The old fellow finished with a look and a sigh, and Doris' subjugation was complete.

Yet she did not let him at this time any further into her plans, possibly because she had not formed any. She only talked on more and more about her love for the young ladies, and her wonder over their conduct, and he, listening for any chance word which might help him in his own perplexity, walked back at her side, till they arrived in sight of the house, when he gave her the pail and slunk back to come on later alone. But a seed was sown at that interview which was destined to bear strange fruit; and it is hard telling which felt the most satisfaction at the understood compact between them— the hard, selfish, and scheming miser, or the weak and obstinate serving-woman, who excused to herself the duplicity of her conduct by the plea, true enough as far as it went, that she was prompted by love for those she served, and a desire to see the two women she admired as bright and happy as their youth and beauty demanded.

XVIII.
SUSPENSE.

The letter which Frank sent to Edgar described his encounter with Huckins, and expressed a wish that the Doctor would employ some proper person to watch his movements and see that he did not make himself disagreeable to the Misses Cavanagh, whom he had evidently set himself to annoy.

What, then, was Etheridge's surprise to receive on the following day a reply from his friend, to the effect that Mr. Huckins had not only called upon the young ladies mentioned by him, but had made himself very much at home with them, having lunched, dined, and report even said breakfasted at their table.

This was startling news to Frank, especially after the letter he had written to Hermione, but he restrained himself from returning at once to Marston, as he was half tempted to do, and wrote her again, this time beseeching her in plain words to have nothing to do with so suspicious a person as he knew this Huckins to be, and advised her where to appeal for assistance in case this intolerable intruder was not willing to be shaken off. This letter brought the following answer:

Dear Mr. Etheridge:

Do not be concerned about us. Mr. Huckins will not trouble us unduly. Knowing his character, we are not likely to be misled by him, and it amuses us in our loneliness to have so queer and surprising a person as our guest.

Aunt Lovell is very sharp and keeps a keen eye upon him. He does not offend us except by his curiosity, but as that is excusable in an old man introduced into a household like ours, we try to make the best of it. When you come yourself we will dismiss the intruder.

Ever sincerely yours,

Hermione Cavanagh.

This letter was put very near Frank's heart, but it did not relieve him from his anxiety. On the contrary, it added to his fears, because it added to his mystification. What did Huckins want of the Misses Cavanagh, and what was the real reason for the indulgence they showed him? Was there a secret in their connection which he ought to know? He began to hasten his business and plan to leave the city again, this time for more than a single night.

Meantime, Dr. Sellick was not without his own secret doubts. Hide it as he would, he still cherished the strongest affection for the once dimpling, dainty, laughing-eyed Emma. Not a day passed but he had to combat a fervent desire to pass her gate, though when he yielded to this temptation he went by like an automaton, and never looked to right or left unless it was dark night. His was a proud soul and an exacting one. His self-esteem had been hurt, and he could not bring himself to make even the shadow of an advance towards one who had been the instrument of his humiliation. And yet he trembled when he thought of misfortune approaching her, and was almost as anxious as Frank about the presence in her house of the hypocritical and unprincipled Huckins. Had he listened only for a moment to the pleading of his better instincts, he would have gone to their door and lent his entreaties to those of Frank for a speedy dismissal of their unreliable guest; but the hour had not yet come for such a self-betrayal, and so he refrained, even while cursing himself for a pride which would not yield even at the impending danger of one so passionately beloved.

He however kept a man at watch upon the suspected stranger, a precaution which certainly did not amount to much, as the danger, if there was any, was not one which a detective stationed outside of the Misses Cavanagh's house would be able to avert.

Meanwhile Huckins, who was in his element, grew more insinuating and fatherly in his manner, day by day. To him this run of a house in which there lurked a mystery worth his penetrating, was a bliss that almost vied with that of feeling himself on the road to wealth. He pottered and poked about in the laboratory, till there was not a spot in the room or an article on the shelves which had not felt the touch of his hand; and Hermione and Emma, with what some might have thought a curious disregard of their father's belongings, let him do this, merely restricting him from approaching their own rooms. Possibly they felt as if some of the gloom of the place was lifted by the presence of even this evil-eyed old man; and possibly the shadows which were growing around them both, as Hermione labored day after day upon the history she was writing for her lover, made this and every other circumstance disconnected with the important theme they were considering, of little moment to them. However that may be, he came and went as he would, and had many sly hours in the long, dim laboratory and in the narrow twisted corridors at the back of the house, and what was worse and perhaps more disastrous still, on the stairs and in the open doorways with Doris, who had learned to toss her head and smile very curiously while busying herself in the kitchen, or taking those brief minutes of respite abroad, which the duties of the place demanded. And so the week passed, and Saturday night came.

It was seven o'clock, and train-time, and the blinds in the Cavanagh house guarding the front windows were tipped just a little. Behind one of these sat Emma, listening to the restless tread of Hermione pacing the floor in the room above. She knew that the all-important letter was done, but she could not know its contents, or what their effect would be upon the free, light-hearted man whose approach they were expecting. She thought she ought to know all that Hermione had been through in the year which had passed, yet the wild words uttered by her sister in their late memorable interview, had left a doubt in her mind which a week's meditations had only served to intensify. Yet the fears to which it had given rise were vague, and she kept saying to herself: "There cannot be anything worse than I know. Hermione exaggerated when she intimated that she had a secret bitterer than that we keep together. She has suffered so much she cannot judge. I will hope that all will go right, and that Mr. Etheridge will receive her explanations and so make her his everlasting debtor. If once she is made to feel that she owes him something, she will gradually yield up her resolve and make both him and me happy. She will see that some vows are better broken than kept, and— —"

Here her thoughts were interrupted by the appearance of Hermione. The latter had not been able to walk off her excitement, and so had come downstairs to bear the moments of suspense with her sister.

"I hope he will not stop," she cried. "I do not feel as if I could see him till— —"

"You will have to," murmured Emma, "for here he comes." And the next moment the ardent, anxious face of the young lawyer appeared at the gate, making the whole outside world seem brighter to one pair of eyes which watched him.

"He wants to talk about our visitor," declared Hermione. "I cannot talk about anything so trivial to-day; so do you see him, and when he rises to go, say that Doris will bring a certain packet to his door to-night. I will not meet his eyes till that ordeal is passed." And with a gasp that showed what this moment was to her, she flew from the room, just as Doris' step was heard in the hall on her way to the front door.

"Where is your sister?" were the first words uttered by Frank, as he came into the room.

"Upstairs," answered Emma. "She does not feel as if she can see you again till everything is clear between you. The letter she promised is written, and you shall have it to-night. Then if you wish to come again— —" her smile completed the sentence.

He took heart at this smile.

"I do not doubt," said he, "that I shall be here very early in the morning." And then he glanced all around him.

"Does Huckins still bother you?" he asked.

"Oh," she cried, with some constraint, "we allow him to come here. 'Tis the least we can do for one— —"

She paused, and seemed to bite off her words.

"Do not let us talk of trivialities," she completed, "till the great question of all is settled. To-morrow, if you come, we will speak of this visitor of whom you so little approve."

"Very well," he rejoined, with some wistfulness, and turned with his usual impetuosity towards the door. "I will go to Dr. Sellick's, then, at once, that I may receive your sister's communication the sooner. Tell her every moment will be an hour till it is in my hands."

"Doris will carry it to you as soon as it is dark. Had we known you were going to stop here, she might have had it ready now. As it is, look for it as I have said, and may it bring you no deeper pain than the mystery of our seclusion has already done. Hermione has noble qualities, and if her temper had never been injured by the accident which befell her in her infancy, there might have been no call for Doris' errand to-night."

"I will remember that," said he, and left the house with the confident smile of a man who feels it impossible to doubt the woman towards whom his heart has gone out in the fullest love.

When the door was shut behind him, Hermione came stealing again down-stairs.

"Does he—is he—prepared to receive the letter?" she asked.

Emma nodded. "I promised that it should go as soon as it is dusk."

"Then send Doris to me in half an hour; and do not try to see me again to-night. I must bear its long and tedious hours alone." And for a second time Hermione disappeared from the room.

In half an hour Doris was sent upstairs. She found Hermione standing in the centre of her room with a thick packet in her hand. She was very pale and her eyes blazed strangely. As Doris advanced she held out the packet with a hand that shook notwithstanding all her efforts to render it firm.

"Take this," she said; "carry it to where Mr. Etheridge stays when here, and place it in his hands yourself, just as you did a former note I entrusted to you."

Doris, with a flush, seized the letter, her face one question, but her lips awed from speaking by the expression of her mistress' face.

"You will do what I say?" asked Hermione.

The woman nodded.

"Go then, and do not wait for an answer; there will be none to-night."

Her gesture of dismissal was imperative and Doris turned to go.

But Hermione had one word more to say. "When you come back," she added, "come to my door and tap on it three times. By that I shall know you have delivered the letter; but you need not come in."

"Very well, Miss," answered the woman, speaking for the first time. And as Hermione turned her back, she gave her young mistress one burning, inquisitive look and then slid out of the room with her eyes on the packet which she almost seemed to devour with her eyes.

As she passed the laboratory door she detected the thin weasel-like face of Huckins looking out.

"What is that?" he whispered, pointing eagerly at the packet.

"Be in the highway at Dobbins' corner, and I'll tell you," she slyly returned, going softly on her way.

And he, with a chuckle which ought to have sounded through that house like a premonition of evil, closed the laboratory door with a careful hand, and descending the twisted staircase which led to the hall below, prepared to follow out her injunction in his own smooth and sneaking way.

"I think I'll spend the evening at the prayer-meeting," he declared, looking in at Emma, as he passed the sitting-room door. "I feel the need of such comfort now and then. Is there anything I can do for either of you up street?"

Emma shook her head; she was glad to be rid of his company for this one evening; and he went out of the front door with a quiet, benevolent air which may not have imposed on her, but which certainly did on Doris, who was watching from the garden to see him go.

They met, as she had suggested, at Dobbins' corner. As it was not quite dark, they walked into a shaded and narrow lane where they supposed themselves to be free from all observation.

"Now tell me," said he, "what your errand is. That it is important I know from the way you look. What is it, good, kind Doris; anything that will help us in our plans?"

"Perhaps," said she. "It is a letter for Mr. Etheridge; see how big and thick it is. It ought to tell a deal, this letter; it ought to explain why she never leaves the house."

The woman's curious excitement, which was made up of curiosity and a real desire to know the secret of what affected her two young mistresses so closely, was quickly communicated to the scheming, eager old man. Taking the packet from her hand, he felt of it with trembling and inquisitive fingers, during which operation it would have been hard to determine upon which face the desire to break the seal was most marked.

"It may contain papers—law papers," he suggested, his thumb and forefinger twitching as they passed over the fastening.

But Doris shook her head.

"No," she declared vivaciously, "there are no law-papers in that envelope. She has been writing and writing for a week. It is her secret, I tell you—the secret of all their queer doings, and why they stay in the house so persistently."

"Then let us surprise that secret," said he. "If we want to help them and make them do like other reasonable folks, we must know with what we have to contend."

"I am sure we would be justified," she rejoined. "But I am afraid Miss Hermione will find us out. Mr. Etheridge will tell her somebody meddled with the fastening."

"Let me take the letter to the hotel, and I will make that all right. It is not the first— —" But here he discreetly paused, remembering that Doris was not yet quite ready to receive the full details of his history.

"But the time? It will take an hour to open and read all there is written here, and Miss Hermione is waiting for me to tell her that I have delivered it to Mr. Etheridge."

"Tell her you had other errands. Go to the stores—the neighbors. She need never know you delivered this last."

"But if you take it I won't know what is in it, and I want to read it myself."

"I will tell you everything she writes. My memory is good, and you shall not miss a word."

"But—but— —"

"It is your only chance," he insinuated; "the young ladies will never tell you themselves."

"I know it; yet it seems a mean thing to do. Can you close the letter so that neither he nor they will ever know it has been opened?"

"Trust me," he leered.

"Hurry then; I will be in front of Dr. Sellick's in an hour. Give me the letter as you go by, and when I have delivered it, meet me on my way back and tell me what she says."

He promised, and hastened with his treasure to the room he still kept at the hotel. She watched him as long as he was in sight and then went about her own improvised errands. Did she realize that she had just put in jeopardy not only her young mistresses' fortunes, but even their lives?

XIX.
A DISCOVERY.

Frank Etheridge waited a long time that night for the promised communication. Darkness came, but no letter; eight o'clock struck, and still there was no sign of the dilatory Doris. Naturally impatient, he soon found this lengthy waiting intolerable. Edgar was busy in his office, or he would have talked to him. The evening paper which he had brought from New York had been read long ago, and as for his cigar, it lacked flavor and all power to soothe him. In his exasperation he went to the book-shelves, and began looking over the numberless volumes ranged in neat rows before him. He took out one, glanced at it, and put it back; he took out another, without even seeing what its title was, looked at it a moment, sighed, and put that back; he took out a third, which opened in his hand at the title-page, saw that it was one of those old-fashioned volumes, designated *The Keepsake*, and was about to close and replace it as he had done the others, when his attention was suddenly and forcibly attracted by a name written in fine and delicate characters on the margin at the top. It was no other than this:

Harriet Smith
Gift of her husband
October 3rd 1848

Harriet Smith! Astounded, almost aghast, he ran to Edgar's office with the volume.

"Edgar! Edgar!" he cried; "look here! See that name! And the book was in your library too. What does it mean? Who was, who is Harriet Smith, that you should have her book?"

Dr. Sellick, taken by surprise, stared at the book a minute, then jumped to his feet in almost as much excitement as Frank himself.

"I got that book from Hermione Cavanagh years ago; there was a poem in it she wanted me to read. I did not know I had the book now. I have never even thought of it from that day to this. Harriet Smith! Yes, that is the name you want, and they must be able to tell you to whom it belongs."

"I believe it; I know it; I remember now that they have always shown an interest in the matter. Hermione wanted to read the will, and—Edgar, Edgar, can they be the heirs for whom we are searching, and is that why Huckins haunts the house and is received by them in plain defiance of my entreaties?"

"If they are the heirs they would have been likely to have told you. Penniless young girls are not usually backward in claiming property which is their due."

"That is certainly true, but this property has been left under a condition. I recollect now how disappointed Hermione looked when she read the will. Give me the book; I must see her sister or herself at once about it." And without heeding the demurs of his more cautious friend, Frank plunged from the house and made his way immediately to the Cavanagh mansion.

His hasty knock brought Emma to the door. As he encountered her look and beheld the sudden and strong agitation under which she labored, he realized for the first time that he was returning to the house before reading the letter upon which so much depended.

But he was so filled with his new discovery that he gave that idea but a thought.

"Miss Cavanagh—Emma," he entreated, "grant me a moment's conversation. I have just found this book in Dr. Sellick's library—a book which he declares was once given him by your sister—and in it——"

They had entered the parlor by this time and were standing by a table upon which burned a lamp——"is a name."

She started, and was bending to look at the words upon which his finger rested, when the door opened. Hermione, alarmed and not knowing what to think of this unexpected return of her lover so soon, as she supposed, after the receipt of her letter, had come down from her room in that mood of extreme tension which is induced by an almost unendurable suspense.

Frank, who in all his experience of her had never seen her look as she did at this moment, fell back from the place where he stood and hastily shook his head.

"Don't look like that," he cried, "or you will make me feel I can never read your letter."

"And have you not read it?" she demanded, shrinking in her turn till she stood on the threshold by which she had entered. "Why then are you here? What could have brought you back so soon when you knew——"

"This," he interpolated hastily, holding up the book which he had let fall on the table at her entrance. "See! the name of Harriett Smith is written in it. Tell me, I pray, why you kept from me so persistently the fact that you knew the person to whom the property I hold in trust rightfully belongs."

The two girls with a quick glance at each other drooped their heads.

"What was the use?" murmured Emma, "since Harriet Smith is dead and her heirs can never claim the property. *We* are her heirs, Mr. Etheridge; Harriet Smith was our mother, married to father thirty-nine years ago after a widowhood of only three months. It was never known in this place that she had had a former husband or had borne the name of Smith. There was so much scandal and unhappiness connected with her first most miserable marriage, that she suppressed the facts concerning it as much as possible. She was father's wife and that was all that the people about here knew."

"I see," said Frank, wondering greatly at this romance in real life.

"But you might have told me," he exclaimed. "When you saw what worriment this case was causing me, you might have informed me that I was expending my efforts in vain."

"I wished to do so," answered Emma, "but Hermione dreaded the arguments and entreaties which would follow."

"I could not bear the thought of them," exclaimed the girl from the doorway where she stood, "any more than I can bear the thought now when a matter of much more importance to me demands your attention."

"I will go," cried Frank. But it was to the empty doorway he spoke; Hermione had vanished with these passionate words.

"She is nearly ill," explained Emma, following him as he made for the door. "You must excuse one who has borne so much."

"I do not excuse her," he cried, "I love her." And the look he cast up the stairs fully verified this declaration. "That is why I go with half on my lips unsaid. To-morrow we will broach the topic again, meanwhile beware of Huckins. He means you no good by being here. Had I known his connection with you, he should never have entered these doors."

"He is our uncle; our mother's brother."

"He is a scamp who means to have the property which is rightfully your due."

"And he will have it, I suppose," she returned. "Hermione has never given me a hope that she means to contend with him in this matter."

"Hermione has had no counsellor but her own will. To-morrow she will have to do with me. But shut the door on Huckins; promise me you will not see him again till after you have seen me."

"I cannot—I know too little what is in that letter."

"Oh, that letter!" he cried, and was gone from the house.

When he arrived at Dr. Sellick's again, he found Doris awaiting him, looking very flushed and anxious. She had a shawl drawn around her, and she held some bundles under that shawl.

"I hope," she said, "that you did not get impatient, waiting for me. I had some errands to do, and while doing them I lost the letter you expected and had to go back and look for it. I found it lying under the counter in Mr. Davis' store and that is why it is so soiled, but the inside is all right, and I can only beg your pardon for the delay."

Drawing the packet from under her shawl, she handed it to the frowning lawyer, her heart standing still as she saw him turn it over and over in his hand. But his looks if angry were not suspicious, and with a relieved nod she was turning to go when he observed:

"I have one word to say to you, Doris. You have told me that you have the welfare of the young ladies you serve at heart. Prove this to be so. If Mr. Huckins comes to the door to-night, or in the early morning, say that Miss Cavanagh is not well and that he had better go to the hotel. Do not admit him; *do not even open the door*, unless Miss Cavanagh or her sister especially command you to do so. He is not a safe friend for them, and I will take the responsibility of whatever you do."

Doris, with wide-stretched eyes and panting breath, paused to collect her faculties. A week ago she would have received this intimation regarding anybody Mr. Etheridge might choose to mention, with gratitude and a certain sense of increased importance. But ambition and the sense of being on intimate and secret terms with a man and bachelor who boasted of his thousands, had made a change in her weak and cunning heart, and she was disposed to doubt the lawyer's judgment of what was good for the young ladies and wise for her.

But she did not show her doubt to one whom she had secretly wronged so lately; on the contrary she bowed with seeming acquiescence, and saying, "Leave me alone to take good care of my young ladies," drew her shawl more closely about her and quietly slid from the house.

A man was standing in the shadow of a great elm on the corner.

As she passed, he whispered: "Don't stop, and don't expect to see me to-night. There is some one watching me, I am sure. To-morrow, if I can I will come."

She had done a wicked and dangerous thing, and she had not learned the secret.

XX.
THE DEVIL'S CAULDRON.

Frank, being left alone, sat down with the letter Doris had given him. These are the words he read:

"Dear Mr. Etheridge:

"I must ask you to walk by my house as early as nine o'clock to-morrow morning. If, having read this letter, you still feel ready to meet fate at my side, you will enter and tell me so. But if the horror that has rested upon my life falls with this reading upon yours, then pass by on the other side, and I will understand your verdict and accept it.

"It was at a very early age that I first felt the blight which had fallen upon my life with the scar which disfigures one side of my face. Such expressions as 'Poor dear! what a pity!'—'She would be very beautiful if it were not for that,' make a deep impression upon a child's mind, especially if that child has a proud and sensitive nature, eager for admiration and shrinking from pity. Emma, who is only a year younger than myself, seemed to me quite an enviable being before I knew what the word envy meant, or why I felt so hot and angry when the neighbors took her up and caressed her, while they only cast looks of compassion at me. I hated her and did not know it; I hated the neighbors, and I hated the places where they met, and the home where I was born. I only loved my mother; perhaps, because she alone never spoke of my misfortune, and when she kissed me did not take pains to choose that side of my face which was without blemish. O my mother! if she had lived! But when I was just fifteen, and was feeling even more keenly than ever what it was to have just missed being the beauty of the town, she died, and I found myself left with only a stern and cruelly abstracted father for guardian, and for companion a sister, who in those days was a girl so merry by nature, and so full of play and sport, that she was a constant source of vexation to me, who hated mirth, and felt aggrieved by a cheerfulness I could not share. These passions of jealousy and pride did not lessen with me as I slowly ripened into womanhood. All our family have been victims of their own indomitable will, and even Emma, gentle as you see her to be now, used to have violent gusts of temper when she was crossed in her plans or pleasures. I never flashed out into bitter speech as she did, or made a noise when I was angry, but I had that slow fire within me which made me perfectly inexorable when I had once made up my mind to any course—no one, not even my father or my sister, having the least influence over me. And so it was that those who knew me began to dread me, even while they were forced to acknowledge that I possessed certain merits of heart and understanding. For the disappointment which had soured my disposition had turned me towards study for relief, and the determination to be brilliant, if I could not be beautiful, came with my maturity, and saved me, perhaps, from being nothing but a burden to my family and friends.

"It was Mr. Lothrop, the Episcopalian minister, who first gave me this turn toward serious pursuits. He was a good man, who had known my mother, and after her death he used to come to the house, and finding me moping in a corner, while Emma made the room gay with her talk, he would draw me out with wonderful stories of women who had become the centre of a great society by the brilliance of their attainments and the sparkle of their wit. Once he called me beautiful, and when he saw the deep flush, which I could not subdue, mantle my cheeks and agitate my whole body, he took me very kindly by the hand, and said:

"'Hermione, you have splendid powers. Perhaps God allowed a little defect to fall upon your beauty, in order to teach you the value of the superior faculties with which you are endowed. You can be a fine, grand woman, if you will.'

"Alas! he did not know that one unconscious tribute to my personal attractions would just then have gone much farther with me than any amount of appreciation for my mental abilities. Yet his words had their effect, and from that moment I began to study—not as my father did, with an absorbed, passionate devotion to one line of thought; that seemed to me narrow and demoralizing, perhaps because almost every disappointment or grief incident to those days could be traced to my father's abstraction to everything disconnected with his laboratory. If I wished to go to the city, or extend my knowledge of the world by travel, it was: 'I have an experiment on hand; I cannot leave the laboratory.' If I wished a new gown, or a set of books, it was: 'I am not rich, and I must use all my spare means in buying the apparatus I need, or the chemicals which are necessary to the discoveries I am in the way of making.' Yet none of those discoveries or experiments ever resulted in anything further than the acquiring on his part of a purely local fame for learning. Therefore no special branch for me, but a general culture which would fit me to shine in any society it might henceforth be my good fortune to enter.

"My father might brood over his books, and bend his back over the retort and crucible; my sister might laugh and attract the liking of a crowd of foolish heads, but I would be the Sevigny, the Rambouillet of my time, and by the eloquence of my conversation and the grace of my manner win for myself that superiority among women which nature had designed for me, but of which cruel fate had robbed me, even before I knew its worth.

"You will say these are great hopes for a village girl who had never travelled beyond her native town, and who knew the great world only through the medium of books. But is it not in villages and quiet sequestered places that lofty ambitions are born? Is it the city boy who becomes the President of our United States, or the city girl who startles the world with her talent as poet, artist, or novelist?

"I read, and learned the world, and felt that I knew my place in it. When my training should be complete, when I had acquired all that my books and the companionship of the best minds in Marston could teach, then I would go abroad, and in the civilization of other lands complete the education which had now become with me a passion, because in it I saw the stepping-stone to the eminence I sought.

"I speak plainly; it is necessary. You must know what was passing in my mind during my girlhood's years, or you will not understand me or the temptations which befell me. Besides, in writing thus I am preparing myself for the revelation of a weakness I have shrunk till now from acknowledging. It must be made. I cannot put it off any longer. I must speak of Dr. Sellick, and explain if possible what he gradually became to me in those lonely and studious years.

"I had known him from a child, but I did not begin to think of him till he began to visit our house. He was a student then, and he naturally took a great interest in chemistry. My father's laboratory was convenient, well-stocked with apparatus, and freely opened to him. To my father's laboratory he accordingly came every day when he was in town, till it began to be quite a matter of course to see him there.

"I was very busy that summer, and for some time looked upon this only as a habit on his part, and so took little heed of his presence. But one day, being weary with the philosophy I had been studying, I took from the shelves a book of poems, and sitting down in the dimmest corner of our stiff old parlor, I began to read some impassioned verses, which, before I knew it, roused my imagination and inflamed my heart to a point which made it easy for any new romantic impression to be made upon me.

"At this instant fate and my ever-cruel destiny brought into my presence Edgar Sellick. He had been like myself hard at work, and had become weary, and anxious perhaps for a change, or, as I am now compelled to think, eager to talk of one whose very existence I was tempted to forget when she was, as then, away from home. He had come into the room where I was, and was standing, flushed and handsome, in the one bright streak of sunlight that flashed at that moment over the floor. I had always liked him, and thought him the only real gentleman in town, but something quite new in my experience made my heart swell as I met his eyes that day, and though I will not call it love (not now), it was something which greatly moved me and made me feel that in the gaze and seeming interest of this man I saw the true road to happiness and to the only life which would ever really satisfy me. For, let it be my excuse, under all my vanity, a vanity greater for the seeming check it had received, dwelt an ardent and irrepressible desire for affection, such affection as I had never received since my dying mother laid her trembling hand upon my head and bade me trust the good God for a happiness I had never possessed. My disfigurement owed its deepest sting to the fact, never revealed to others before, and scarcely acknowledged to myself then, that it stood in the way, as I thought, to my ever being passionately beloved. When, therefore, I saw the smile on Dr. Sellick's face, and realized that he was looking for me, I rose up with new hopes in my heart and a new brightness in my life.

"But we said nothing, he or I, beyond the merest commonplaces, and had my powers of observation been as keen then as they are now, since a new light has been shed upon those days, I would have perceived that his eye did not brighten when it rested upon me, save when some chance mention was made of Emma, and of the pleasures she was enjoying abroad. But no doubts came to me at that time. Because my heart was warm I took it for granted that his was so also, and not dreaming of any other reason for his attentions than the natural one of his desiring my society for its own sake, I gradually gave myself up to a feeling of which it is shame now for me to speak, but which, as it was the origin of all my troubles, I must compel myself to acknowledge here in all its force and fervor.

"The fact that he never uttered a word of love or showed me any attention beyond that of being constantly at my side, did not serve to alarm or even dispirit me. I knew him to have just started upon his career as physician, and also knew him to be proud, and was quite content to cherish my hopes and look towards a future that had unaccountably brightened into something very brilliant indeed.

"It was while matters were in this condition that Emma came home from her trip. I remember the occasion well, and how pretty she looked in her foreign gowns. You, who have only seen her under a shadow, cannot imagine how pleasing she was, fresh from her happy experiences abroad, and an ocean trip, which had emphasized the roses on her cheek and the brightness in her eyes. But though I saw it all and felt that I could never compete with the gaiety which was her charm, I did not feel that old sickly jealousy of her winsome ways which once distorted her figure in my eyes, nor did I any longer hate her laugh or shrink from her merry banter. For I had my own happiness, as I thought, and could afford to be lenient towards a gay young thing who had no secret hope like mine to fill her heart and make it too rich with joy for idle mirth.

"It was a gay season for humble little Marston, and various picnics followed by a ball in Hartford promised festivities enough to keep us well alive. I did not care for festivities, but I did care for Dr. Sellick, and picnics and balls offered opportunities beyond those given by his rather commonplace visits to the house. I therefore looked forward to the picnics at the seashore with something like expectancy, and as proof of my utter blindness to the real state of affairs, it never even entered into my head that it would be the scene of his first meeting with Emma after an absence of many months.

"Nor did any behavior on his part at this picnic enlighten me as to his true feelings, or the direction in which they ran. He greeted Emma in my presence, and the unusual awkwardness with which he took her hand told me nothing, though it may have whispered something to her. I only noticed that he had the most refined features and the most intellectual head of any one present, and was very happy thereat, and disposed to accord him an interview if he showed any inclination to draw me away from the rest of the merry-makers. But he did not, though he strolled several times away by himself; and once I saw him chatting with Emma; but this fact made no impression upon me and my Fool's Paradise remained still intact.

"But that night on reaching home I felt that something was going wrong. Aunt Lovell was then with us, and I saw her cast a glance of dismay upon me as I entered the room where she and Emma had been closeted together. Emma, too, looked out of sorts, and hardly spoke to me when I passed her in the hall. Indeed, that quick temper of which I have already spoken was visible in her eyes, and if I had opened my own lips I am sure she would have flashed out with some of her bitter speeches. But I was ignorant of having given her any cause for anger; so, thinking she was jealous of the acquirements which I had made in her absence, and the advantages they now gave me in any gathering where cultured people came together, I hurried by her in some disdain, and in the quiet of my own room regained the equanimity my aunt's look and Emma's manifest ill-feeling towards me had for a moment shaken.

"It was the last time I was to encounter anger in that eye. When I met her next morning I discovered that some great change had passed over her. The high spirits I had always secretly deprecated were gone, and in their place behold an indescribable gentleness of manner which has never since forsaken her.

"But this was not all; her attitude towards me was different. From indifference it had budded into love; and if one can become devoted in a night, then was it devotion that she showed in every look and every word she bestowed upon me from that day. The occasion for this change I did not then know; when I did, a change passed over me also.

"Meantime a grave event took place. I was out walking, and my path took me by the church. I mean the one that stands by itself on the top of the hill. Perhaps you have been there, perhaps you have not. It is a lonesome-looking structure, but it has pleasant surroundings, while the view of the sea which you get from its rear is superb. I often used to go there, just for the breath of salt-water that seemed to hover about the place, and as there was a big flat stone in the very spot most favorable for observation, I was accustomed to sit there for hours with my book or pencil for company.

"Had Edgar Sellick loved me he would have been acquainted with my habits. This is apparent to me now, but then I seemed to see nothing beyond my own wishes and hopes. But this does not explain what happened to me there. I was sitting on the stone of which I have spoken, and was looking at the long line of silver light on the horizon which we call the sea, when I suddenly heard voices. Two men were standing on the other side of the church, engaged, in all probability, in gazing at the landscape, but talking on a subject very remote from what they saw before them. I heard their words distinctly. They were these:

"'I tell you she is beautiful.'

"I did not recognize the voice making use of this phrase, but the one that answered was well known to me, and its tones went through me like a knife.

"'Oh, yes, if you only see one side of her face.'

"They were speaking of me, and the last voice, careless, indifferent, almost disdainful as it was, was that of Edgar Sellick.

"I quailed as at a mortal blow, but I did not utter a sound. I do not know as I even moved; but that only shows the control a woman unconsciously holds over herself. For nothing short of a frenzied scream could have voiced the agony I felt, or expressed the sudden revolt which took place within me, sickening me at once with life, past, present, and future. Not till they had strolled away did I rise and dash down the hill into the wood that lies at its foot, but when I felt myself alone and well shielded from the view of any chance observer, I groaned again and again, and wrung my hands in a misery to which I can do but little justice now. I had been thrust so suddenly out of paradise. I had been so sure of *his* regard, *his* love. The scar which disfigured me in other eyes had been, as I thought, no detriment in his. He loved me, and saw nothing in me but what was consistent with that love. And now I heard him with my own ears speak contemptuously of that scar. All that I had hoped, all that I had confided in, was gone from me in an instant, and I felt myself toppling into a misery I could neither contemplate nor fathom. For an hour I walked the paths of that small wood, communing with myself; then I took my resolve. Life, which had brought me nothing but pain and humiliation, was not worth living. The hopes I had indulged, the love in which I had believed, had proved a mockery, and the shame which their destruction brought was worse than death, and so to be more shunned than death. I was determined to die.

"The means were ready to my hand. Further on in that very wood I knew of a pool. It was a deep, dark, deadly place, as its name of Devil's Cauldron betokens, and in it I felt I could most fitly end the life that was dear to no one. I began to stray towards that place. As I went I thought of home, but with no feelings of longing or compunction. Emma might be kind, had been kind for the last day or so, but Emma did not love me, would not sacrifice anything for me, would not grieve, save in the decent way her sisterhood would naturally require. As for my father, he would feel the interruption it would cause in his experiments, but that would not last long, and in a few days he would be again in his beloved laboratory. No one, not a single being, unless it was dear Aunt Lovell, would sincerely mourn me or sigh over the death of the poor girl with a scar. Edgar Sellick might raise his eyebrows in some surprise, and Edgar Sellick should know what a careless word could do. I had a pencil and paper in my pocket, and I meant to use them. He should not go through life happy and careless, when a line from me would show him that the death of one who had some claims upon his goodness, lay at his door.

"The sight of the dim, dark pool did not frighten me from these intentions. I was in that half-maddened state of disgust and shame which makes the promise of any relief look inviting and peaceful. I loved the depth of that cool, clear water. I saw in it rest, peace, oblivion. Had I not had that letter to write I would have tasted that rest and peace, and these words would never have come to your eyes. But the few minutes I took to write some bitter and incoherent lines to Dr. Sellick saved me from the doom I contemplated. Have I reason to be thankful it was so? To-morrow morning will tell me.

"The passion which guided my pencil was still in my face when I laid the paper down on the bank and placed a stone above it. The eyes which saw those evidences of passion were doubtless terrified by them, for as I passed to the brink of the pool and leaned over it I felt a frenzied grasp on my arm, and turning, I met the look of Emma fixed upon me in mortal terror and apprehension.

"'What are you going to do?' she cried. 'Why are you leaning over the Devil's Cauldron like that?'

"I had not wished to see her or to say good-by to any one. But now, that by some unaccountable chance she had come upon me, in my desperation I would give her one kiss before I went to my doom.

"'Emma,' I exclaimed, meeting her look without any sharp sense of shame, 'life is not as promising for me as it is for you; life is not promising for me at all, so I seek to end it.'

"The horror in her eyes deepened. The grasp on my arm became like that of a man.

"'You are mad,' she cried. 'You do not know what you are doing. What has happened to drive you to a deed like this? I—I thought—' and here she stammered and lost for the moment her self-control—'that you seemed very happy last night.'

"'I was,' I cried. 'I did not know then what a blighted creature I was. I thought some one might be brought to love me, even with this frightful, hideous scar on my face. But I know now that I am mistaken; that no man will ever overlook this; that I must live a lonely life, a suffering life; and I have not the strength or the courage to do so. I—I might have been beautiful,' I cried, 'but——'

"Her face, suddenly distorted by the keenest pain, drew my attention, even at that moment of immeasurable woe, and made me stop and say in less harsh and embittered tones:

"'No one will miss me very much, so do not seek to stop me.'

"Her head fell forward, her eyes sought the ground, but she did not loosen her hold on my arm. Instead of that, it tightened till it felt like a band of steel.

"'You have left a letter there,' she murmured, allowing her eyes to wander fearfully towards it. 'Was it to me? to our father?'

"'No,' I returned.

"She shuddered, but her eyes did not leave the spot. Suddenly her lips gave a low cry; she had seen the word *Sellick.*

"'Yes,' I answered in response to what I knew were her thoughts. 'It is that traitor who is killing me. He has visited me day by day, he has followed me from place to place; he has sought me, smiled upon me, given me every token of love save that expressed in words; and now, now I hear him, when he does not know I am near, speak disrespectfully of my looks, of this scar, as no man who loves, or ever will love, could speak of any defect in the woman he has courted.'

"'You did not hear aright,' came passionately from her lips. 'You are mistaken. Dr. Sellick could not so far forget himself.'

"'Dr. Sellick can and did. Dr. Sellick has given me a blow for which his fine art of healing can find no remedy. Kiss me, Emma, kiss me, dear girl, and do not hold me so tight; see, we might tumble into the water together.'

"'And if we did,' she gasped, 'it would be better than letting you go alone. No, no, Hermione, you shall never plunge into that pool while I live to hold you back. Listen to me, listen. Am I nothing to you? Will you not live for me? I have been careless, I know, happy in my own hopes and pleasures, and thinking too little, oh, much too little, of the possible griefs or disappointments of my only sister. But this shall be changed; I promise you shall all be changed. I will live for you henceforth; we will breathe, work, suffer, enjoy together. No sister shall be tenderer, no lover more devoted than I will be to you. If you do not marry, then will not I. No pleasure that is denied you shall be accepted by me. Only come away from this dark pool; quit casting those glances of secret longing into that gruesome water. It is too awful, too loathsome a place to swallow so much beauty; for you are beautiful, no matter what any one says; so beautiful that it is almost a mercy you have some defect, or we should not dare to claim you for our own, you are so far above what any of us could hope for or expect.'

"But the bitterness that was in my soul could not be so easily exorcised.

"'You are a good girl,' I said, 'but you cannot move me from my purpose.' And I tried to disengage myself from her clasp.

"But the young face, the young form which I had hitherto associated only with what was gay, mirthful, and frivolous, met me with an aspect which impressed even me and made me feel it was no child I had to deal with but a woman as strong and in a state of almost as much suffering as myself.

"'Hermione,' she cried, 'if you throw yourself into that pool, I shall follow you. I will not live ten minutes after you. Do you know why? Because I—*I* caused you that scar which has been the torment of your life. It was when we were children—babes, and I have only known it since last night. Auntie Lovell told me, in her sympathy for you and her desire to make me more sisterly. The knowledge has crushed me, Hermione; it has made me hate myself and love you. Nothing I can do now can ever atone for what I did then; though I was so young, it was anger that gave me strength to deal the blow which has left this indelible mark behind it. Isn't it terrible? I the one to blame and you the one to suffer!—But there must be no dying, Hermione, no dying, or I shall feel myself a murderess. And you do not want to add that horror to my remorse, now that I am old enough to feel remorse, and realize your suffering. You will be a little merciful and live for my sake if not for your own.'

"She was clinging to me, her face white and drawn, upturned towards mine with pitiful pleading, but I had no words with which to comfort her, nor could I feel as yet any relenting in my fixed purpose. Seeing my unmoved look she burst into sobs, then she cried suddenly:

"'I see I must prepare to die too. But not to-day, Hermione. Wait a month, just one month, and then if you choose to rush upon your fate, I will not seek to deter you, I will simply share it; but not to-day, not in this rush of maddened feeling. Life holds too much,—may yet give you too much, for any such reckless disregard of its prospects. Give it one chance, then, and me one chance—it is all I ask. One month of quiet waiting and then—decision.'

"I knew no month would make any difference with me, but her passionate pleading began to work upon my feelings.

"'It will be a wretched time for me,' said I, 'a purgatory which I shall be glad to escape.'

"'But for my sake,' she murmured, 'for my sake; I am not ready to die yet, and your fate—I have said it—shall be mine.'

"'For your sake then,' I cried, and drew back from the dangerous brink upon which we had both been standing. 'But do not think,' I added, as we paused some few feet away, 'that because I yield now, I will yield then. If after a month of trying to live, I find myself unable, I shall not consult you, Emma, as to my determination, any more than I shall expect you to embrace my doom because in the heat of your present terror you have expressed your intention of doing so.'

"'Your fate shall be my fate, as far as I myself can compass it,' she reiterated. And I, angry at what I thought to be an unwarrantable attempt to put a check upon me, cried out in as bitter a tone as I had ever used:

"'So be it,' and turned myself towards home."

XXI.
IN THE LABORATORY.

"ButEmma, with a careful remembrance of what was due to my better nature, stopped to pick up the letter I had left lying under a stone, and joining me, placed it in my hand, by which it was soon crumpled up, torn, and scattered to the wind. As the last bits blew by us, we both sighed and the next minute walked rapidly towards home.

"You will say that all this was experience enough for one day, but fate sometimes crowds us with emotions and eventful moments. As we entered the house, I saw auntie waiting for us at the top of the first stairs; and when she beckoned to Emma only, I was glad—if I could be glad of anything—that I was to be left for a few minutes to myself. Turning towards a little crooked staircase which leads to that part of the house containing my own room and my father's laboratory, I went wearily up, feeling as if each step I took dragged a whole weight of woe behind it.

"I was going to my own room, but as I passed the open laboratory door, I perceived that the place was empty, and the fancy took me, I know not why, to go in. I had never liked the room, it was so unnaturally long, so unnaturally dismal, and so connected with the pursuits I had come to detest. Now it had an added horror for me. Here Dr. Sellick had been accustomed to come, and here was the very chair in which he had sat, and the table at which he had worked. Why, then, with all this old and new shrinking upon me did I persistently cross the threshold and darken my already clouded spirit with the torturing suggestions I found there? I do not know. Perhaps my evil spirit lured me on; perhaps—I am beginning to believe in a Providence now—God had some good purpose in leading me to fresh revelations, though up to this time they have seemed to cause me nothing but agony and shame.

"No one was in the room, I say, and I went straight to its middle window. Here my father's desk stood, for he used the room for nearly every purpose of his life. I did not observe the desk; I did not observe anything till I turned to leave; then I caught sight of a letter lying on the desk, and stopped as if I had been clutched by an iron hand, for it was an open letter, and the signature at the bottom of the sheet was that of Edgar Sellick.

"'Can I never escape from that man?' thought I, and turned passionately away. But next minute I found myself bending over it, devouring it first with my eyes, and then taking it to my heart, for it was an expression of love for the daughter of the man to whom it was addressed, and that man was my father.

"This language as I now know referred to Emma, and she was under no error in regard to it, nor was my father nor my aunt. But I thought it referred to me, and as I read on and came upon the sentence in which he asked, as I supposed, for my hand and the privilege of offering himself to me at the coming ball, I experienced such a revulsion of feeling that I lost all memory of the words I had overheard him speak, or attributed them to some misunderstanding on my part, which a word or look from him could easily explain.

"Life bloomed for me again, and I was happy, madly happy for a few short moments. Even the horrible old room I was in seemed cheerful, and I was just acknowledging to myself that I should have made a great mistake if I had carried out my wicked impulse toward self-destruction, when my father came in. He shrank back when he saw me; but I thought nothing of that; I did not even wonder why Emma was closeted with aunt. I only thought of the coming ball, and the necessity of preparing myself for it right royally.

"I had come from the desk, and was crossing the floor to go out. My happiness made me turn.

"'Father,' said I, taking what I thought to be an arch advantage of the situation; 'may I not have a new dress for the ball?'

"He paused, cast a glance at his desk, and then another at me. He had been, though I did not know it, in conversation with Emma and my aunt, and was more alive to the matters of the hour than usual. It was therefore with some display of severity that he confronted me and said:

"'You are not going to the ball, Hermione.'

"Struck as by a blow, the more severely that it was wholly unexpected, I gasped:

"'Not going to the ball when you know what depends upon it? Do you not like Dr. Sellick, father?'

"He mumbled something between his lips, and advancing to the desk, took up the letter which he thus knew I had read, and ostentatiously folded it.

"'I like Dr. Sellick well enough,' was his reply, 'but I do not approve of balls, and desire you to keep away from them.'

"'But you said we might go,' I persisted, suspecting nothing, seeing nothing in this but a parent's unreasonable and arbitrary display of power.

'Why have you changed your mind? Is it because Dr. Sellick has fixed upon that time for making me the offer of his hand?'

"'Perhaps,' his dry lips said.

"Angry as I had never been in all my life, I tried to speak, and could not. Had I escaped suicide to have my hopes flung in this wanton way again to the ground, and for no reason that I or any one else could see?'

"'But you acknowledge,' I managed at last to stammer, 'that you like him.'

"'That is not saying I want him for a son-in-law.'

"'Whom do you want?' I cried. 'Is there any one else in town superior to him in wit or breeding? If he loves me——'

"My father's lip curled.

"'He says he does,' I flashed out fiercely.

"'You should not have read my letters,' was all my father replied.

"I was baffled, exasperated, at my wits' end; all the more that I saw his eye roaming impatiently towards the pneumatic trough where some hydrogen gas was collecting for use.

"'Father, father,' I cried, 'be frank to me. What are your objections to Dr. Sellick? He is your friend; he works with you; he is promising in his profession; he has every qualification but that of wealth——'

"'That is enough,' broke in my father.

"I looked at him in dismay and shrank back. How could I know he was honestly trying to save me from a grief and shame they all thought me unequal to meeting. I saw nothing but his cold smile, heard nothing but his harsh words.

"'You are cruel; you are heartless,' burst from me in a rage. 'You never have shown the least signs of a mercenary spirit before, and now you make Dr. Sellick's lack of money an excuse for breaking my heart.'

"'Hermione,' my father slowly rejoined, 'you have a frightful temper. You had better keep down the exhibitions of it when you are in this room.'

"'This room!' I repeated, almost beside myself. 'This grave rather of every gentle feeling and tender thought which a father should have towards a most unfortunate child. If you loved me but half as well as you love these old jars——'

"But here his face, usually mild in its abstraction, turned so pale and hard that I was frightened at what I had said.

"'Hermione,' he cried, 'there is no use trying to show you any consideration. Know the truth then; know that——'

"Why did he not go on? Why was he not allowed to tell me what I may have been but little fitted to hear, but which if I had heard it at that time would have saved me from many grave and fatal mistakes. I think he would have spoken; I think he meant to tell me that Dr. Sellick's offer was for Emma, and not for me, but Emma herself appeared just then at the door, and though I did not detect the gesture she made, I gather that it was one of entreaty from the way he paused and bit his lip.

"'It is useless to talk,' he exclaimed. 'I have said that you are to stay home from the ball. I also say that you are not to accept or refuse Dr. Sellick's addresses. I will answer his letter, and it will not be one of acceptance.'

"Why did I not yield to his will and say nothing? When I saw how everything was against me, why did I not succumb to circumstances, and cease to maintain a struggle I knew then to be useless? Because it was not in my nature to do so; because Providence had given me an indomitable will which had never been roused into its utmost action till now. Drawing myself up till I felt that I was taller than he, I advanced with all the fury of suppressed rage, and quietly said the fatal words which, once uttered, I never knew how to recall:

"'If you play the tyrant, I will not play the part of submissive slave. Keep me here if you will; restrain me from going where my fancy and my desires lead, and I will obey you. But, father, if you do this, if you do not allow me to go to the ball, meet Dr. Sellick, and accept his offer, then mark me, I will never go out of this house again. Where you keep me I will stay till I am carried out a corpse, and no one and nothing shall ever make me change my mind.'

"He stared, laughed, then walked away to his pneumatic trough. 'Suit yourself about that,' said he, 'I have nothing to do with your whims.' Probably he thought I was raving and would forget my words before the day was out.

"But there was another person present who knew me better, and I only realized what I had done when I beheld Emma's slight body lying insensible at my feet."

XXII.
STEEL MEETS STEEL.

Up to this point Frank had read with an absorption which precluded the receiving of all outward impressions. But the secret reached, he drew a long breath and became suddenly conscious of a lugubrious sound breaking in upon the silence with a gloomy iteration which was anything but cheering.

The fog-horn was blowing out on Dog Island.

"I could have done without that accompaniment," thought he, glancing at the sheets still before him. "It gives me a sense of doom."

But the fog was thick on the coast and the horn kept on blowing.

Frank took up the remaining sheets.

"Life for me was now at an end indeed, and not for me only, but for Emma. I had not meant to involve her in my fate. I had forgotten her promise, *forgotten*. But when I saw her lying there I remembered, and a sharp pang pierced me for all my devouring rage. But I did not recall my words, I could not. I had uttered them with a full sense of what they meant to me, and the scorn with which they were received only deepened my purpose to keep the threat I had made. Can you understand such a disposition, and can you continue to love the possessor of it?

"My father, who was shocked at Emma's fall, knowing better than I did perhaps the real misery which lay behind it, cast me a look which did not tend to soften my obduracy, and advanced to pick her up. When he had carried her to her own room, I went proudly to mine, and such was the depth of my anger and the obstinate nature of my will that I really felt better able to face the future now that I had put myself into a position requiring pride and purpose to sustain it. But I did feel some relenting when I next saw Emma— such a change was visible in her manner. Meekness had taken the place of the merriment which once made the house to ring, and the eye which once sparkled now showed sadness and concern. I did not, however suspect she had given up anything but freedom, and though this was much, as I very soon began to find, I was not yet by any means so affected by her devotion, that I could do more than beg her to reconsider her own determination and break a promise from which I would be only too happy to release her.

"But the answer with which she always met my remonstrances was, 'Your fate shall be my fate. When it becomes unbearable to us both you will release me by releasing yourself.' Which answer always hardened me again, for I did not wish to be forced to think that the breaking up of our seclusion rested with me, or that anything but a relenting on my father's part could make any change in my conduct.

"Meanwhile that father maintained towards me an air of the utmost indifference. He worked at his experiments as usual, came and went through the sombre house, which was unrelieved now by Emma's once bright sallies and irrepressible laughter, and made no sign that he saw any difference in it or us. Aunt Lovell alone showed sympathy, and when she saw that sympathy accomplished nothing, tried first persuasion and then argument.

"But she had iron and steel to deal with and she soon ceased her gentle efforts, and as the time of her visit was drawing to a close, returned again to those gentle expressions of silent sympathy more natural to her nature; and so the first week passed.

"We had determined, Emma and I, that no one beside our four selves should ever know the secret of our strange behavior. Neighbors might guess, gossips might discuss it, but no one should ever know why we no longer showed ourselves in the street, went to any of the social gatherings of the place, or attended the church from which we had never before been absent. When, therefore, the ball came off and we were not seen there, many were the questions asked, and many were the surmises uttered, but we did not betray our secret, nor was it for some time after this that the people about us awoke to the fact that we no longer left our home.

"What happened when this fact was fully realized, I will not pause to relate, for matters of a much more serious nature press upon me and I must now speak of the bitter and terrible struggle which gradually awoke between my father and myself. He had as I have already related, shown nothing at first but indifference, but after the first week had passed he suddenly seemed to realize that I meant what I said. The result was a conflict between us from the effects of which I am still suffering.

"The first intimation I received of his determination to make me break my word came on a Sunday morning. He had been in his room dressing for church, and when he came out he rapped at my door and asked if I were ready to go with him.

"Naturally I flung wide the door and let him see my wrathful figure in its morning dress.

"'Can you ask,' I cried, 'when you yourself have made it impossible for me to enjoy anything outside of this house, even the breath of fresh air to which all are entitled?'

"He looked as if he would like to strike me, but he did not—only smiled. If I could have known all that lay under that smile, or been able to fathom from what I knew of my own stubborn nature, the terrible depths which its sarcasm barely suggested!

"'You would be a fool if you were not so wicked,' was all he said, and shuffled away to my sister's door.

"In a few minutes he came back.

"'Hermione,' he cried, 'put on your hat and come directly with me to church.'

"I simply looked at him.

"'Do you hear?' he exclaimed, stepping into the room and shutting the door after him. 'I have had enough of this nonsense, and to-day you go out with me to church or you never shall call me father again.'

"'Have you been a father to me?' I asked.

"He shook and quivered and was a picture of rage. I remembered as I looked at him, thinking, 'Behold the source of my own temper,' but I said nothing, and was in no other way affected by what I saw.

"'I have been such a father to you as your folly and blindness deserved,' he exclaimed. 'Should I continue to treat you according to your deserts, I would tell you what would lay you in shame at my feet. But I have promised to be silent, and silent will I be, not out of consideration for you, but because your punishment will some day be the greater. Will you give up this whim and go with me, and so let your sister go also, or will you not?'

"'I will not.'

"He showed a sudden change of manner. 'I will ask you the same question next Sunday,' said he, and left my presence with his old air of indifference and absorption. No subject disconnected with his work could rouse more than a temporary passion in him.

"He kept his word. Every Sunday morning he came on the same errand to my door, and every Sunday he went forth alone. During the week days he did not trouble me. Indeed, I do not know as he thought of me then, or even of Emma, who had always been dearer to him than I. He was engaged on some new experiment, some vital discovery that filled him with enthusiasm and made every moment passed out of his laboratory a trial and a loss to him. He ate that he might work, he slept that he might gather new strength and inspiration for the next day. If visitors came he refused to see them; the one visitor who could have assisted him at the retort and crucible had been denied the door, and any other was a hindrance. Our troubles, our cares, our schemes, or our attempts to supply the table and dress ourselves upon the few and fewer dollars he now allowed us, sank into insignificance before the one idea with which he was engrossed. I do not think he even knew when we ceased having meat for dinner. That Emma was growing pale and I desperate did not attract his attention as much as a speck of dust upon a favorite jar or a crack in one of his miserable tubes.

"That this deep absorption of his was real and not assumed was made evident to me the first Sunday morning he forgot to come to my door. It was a relief not to have to go through the usual formula, but it alarmed me too. I was afraid I was to be allowed to go my own way unhindered, and I was beginning to feel a softness towards Emma and a longing for the life of the world, which made me anxious for some excuse to break a resolution which was entailing upon me so much more suffering than I had anticipated. Indeed, I think if my father had persisted in his practice and come but two or three Sunday mornings more to my door, that my pride would have yielded at last, and my feet in spite of me have followed him out of a house that, since it had become my prison, had become more than ever hateful to me. But he stopped just as a crisis was taking place in my feelings, and my heart hardened again. Before it could experience again the softening effects of Emma's uncomplaining presence the news came that Dr. Sellick had left the town, and my motive for quitting the house was taken from me. Henceforth I felt no more life or hope or ambition than if I had been an automaton.

"This mood received one day a startling interruption. As I was sitting in my room with a book in my hand I felt too listless to read, the door opened, and my father stood before me. As it was weeks since he had appeared on a Sunday morning and months since he had showed himself there on a week day, I was startled, especially as his expression was more eager and impatient than I had ever seen it except when he was leaning over his laboratory table. Was his heart touched at last? Had he good news for me, or was he going to show his fatherhood once more by proffering me an invitation to go out with him in a way which my pride would allow me to accept? I rose in a state of trembling agitation, and made up my mind that if he spoke kindly I would break the hideous bonds which held me and follow him quickly into the street.

"But the words which fell from his lips drove every tender impulse back into my heart.

"'Have you any jewels, Hermione? I think I gave your mother some pearls when we were married. Have you them? I want them if you have.'

"The revulsion of feeling was too keen. Quivering with disappointment, I cried out, bitterly:

"'What to do? To give us bread? We have not had any too much of it lately.'

"He stared, but did not seem to take in my words.

"'Fetch the pearls,' he cried; 'I cannot afford to waste time like this; my experiments will suffer.'

"'And have you no eye, no heart,' I asked, 'for the sufferings of your daughters? With no motive but an arbitrary love of power, you robbed me of my happiness. Now you want my jewels; the one treasure I have left either in the way of value, or as a remembrance of the mother who loved me.'

"Of all this he heard but one word.

"'Are they valuable?' he asked. 'I had hoped so, but I did not know. Get them, child, get them. The discovery upon which my fame may rest will yet be made.'

"'Father, father, you want to sell them,' I screamed. 'My mother's jewels; my dead mother's jewels!'

"He looked at me; this protest had succeeded in entering his ears, and his eye, which had been simply eager, became all at once dangerous.

"'I do not care whose they were,' he hissed, 'so long as they are now mine. It is money I want, and money I will have, and if they will get it for me you had better be thankful. Otherwise I shall have to find some other way to raise it.'

"I was cowed; he did not say what other way, but I knew by his look I had better not drive him into it, so I went to the place where I kept these sacred relics, and taking them out, laid them in his trembling, outstretched hand.

"'Are these all?' he asked. And I wondered, for he had never shown the least shrewdness in any matter connected with money before.

"'All but a trivial little locket which Emma wears,' said I.

"'Is it worth much?'

"'Scarcely five dollars,' I returned.

"'Five dollars would buy the bit of platinum I want,' he muttered. But he did not ask for the locket, for I saw it on Emma's neck the next day.

"This was the beginning of a fresh struggle. My father begrudged us everything: the food we ate; the plain, almost homely, clothes we wore. He himself wellnigh starved his own body, and when in the midst of an experiment, his most valuable retort broke in his hand, you could have heard his shriek of dismay all over the house. The following Sunday he did not go to church; he no longer had a coat to wear; he had sold his only broadcloth suit to a wandering pedlar.

"Our next shock was the dismissal of the man who had always kept our garden in order. Doris would have been sent away also, but that father knew this would mean a disorder in the household which might entail interruption in his labors. He did not dare to leave himself to the tender mercies of his daughters. But her pay was stopped.

"Meanwhile his discovery delayed. It was money that he needed, he said, more money, much more money. He began to sell his books. In the midst of this a stranger came to visit him, and now the real story of my misery begins."

XXIII.
A GROWING HORROR.

"Thereare some men who fill you from the beginning with a feeling of revulsion. Such a one was Antony Harding. When he came into the parlor where I sat, I felt it difficult to advance and greet him with the necessary formalities, so forcibly did I shrink from his glance, his smile, his bow of easy assurance. Not that he was ugly of feature, or possessed of any very distinguishing marks in face or form to render him personally repulsive. He was what some might have called good-looking, and many others a gentlemanly-appearing man. But to me he was simply revolting, and I could not then or now tell why, for, as far as I know, he has never done anything incompatible with his standing as a gentleman and a man of family and wealth.

"He had some claim upon my father, and desired very much to see him. I, who could not dispute that claim, was going to call my father, when Mr. Harding stopped me, thinking, I really believe, that he would not see me again, and I was forced, greatly against my will, to stand and answer some half-dozen innocent enough questions, while his eyes roamed over my features and took in the scar I turned towards him as a sort of defence. Then he let me go, but not before I saw in him the beginning of that fever which made me for a while hate the very name of love.

"With a sense of disgust quite new to me, I rushed from the room to the laboratory. The name by which he had introduced himself was a strange one to me, and I had no idea my father would see him. But as soon as I uttered the word Harding, the impatience with which he always met any interruption gave way to a sudden and irresistible joy, and, jumping up from his seat, he cried:

"'Show him up! show him up. He is a rich man and interested in chemistry. He cannot but foresee the fame which awaits the man who brings to light the discovery I am seeking.'

"'He says he has some claim on you,' I murmured, anything but pleased at this prospect of seeing a man whose presence I so disliked, inveigled into matters which might demand his reappearance in the house.

"'Claims? claims? Perhaps he has; I cannot remember. But send him up; I shall soon make him forget any claims he may have.'

"I did as my father bade me. I sent the smiling, dapper, disagreeably attentive man to the laboratory, and when this was done, went to the window and threw it up with some vague idea of cleansing the room from an influence which stifled me.

"You may imagine then with what a sense of apprehension I observed that my father fairly glowed with delight when he came to the supper-table. From being the half-sullen, half-oblivious companion who had lately chilled our board and made it the scene of anything but cheer or comfort, he had brightened at once into a garrulous old man, ready with jests and full of condescending speeches in regard to his great experiments. Emma, to whom I had said nothing, looked her innocent pleasure at this, and both of us started in amazement when he suddenly turned towards me, and surveyed me with something like interest and pleasurable curiosity.

"'Why do you look at me like that?' I could not help saying. 'I should think you had never seen me before, father.'

"'Perhaps I never have,' he laughed. Then quite seriously: 'I was looking to see if you were as handsome as Mr. Harding said you were. He told me he had never seen so beautiful a woman in his life.'

"I was shocked; more than that, I was terrified; I half-rose from the table, and forgetting everything else which made my life a burden to me, I had some wild idea of rushing from the house, from the town, anywhere to escape the purpose I perceived forming itself in my father's mind.

"'Father,' I cried, with a trembling in my tones that was not common to them, even in the moments of my greatest displeasure; 'I hate that man, and abominate the very idea of his presuming to admire me. Do not ever mention him to me again. It makes my very soul turn sick.'

"It was an unwise speech; it was the unwisest speech I could have made. I felt this to be so the moment I had spoken, and stole a look of secret dismay at Emma, who sat quite still and helpless, gazing, in silent consternation, from my father to myself.

"'You will hate no one who can help me perfect my experiments,' he retorted. 'If I command you to do so, you must even love him, though we have not got so far as that yet.'

"'I will never love anybody again,' I answered bitterly. 'And I would not love this man if your discoveries and my own life even hung upon it.'

"'You would not?' He was livid now. 'Well, we shall see. He is coming here to dinner to-morrow, and if you dare to show him anything but the respect due to an honored guest you will live to rue it as you have never rued anything yet.'

"Threats that are idle on some lips are anything but idle on ours, as I think you have already begun to perceive. I therefore turned pale and said no more, but all night the tormenting terror was upon me, and when the next day came I was but little fitted to sustain the reputation for beauty which I had so unfortunately earned from a distasteful man's lips the day before.

"But Antony Harding was not one to easily change his first impressions. He had made up his mind that I was beautiful, and he kept to that opinion to the last. I had dressed myself in my most expensive but least becoming gown, and I wore my hair in a way to shock the taste of most men. But I saw from the first moment that his eyes fell on my face that this made no difference to him, and that I must take other means to disillusionize him. So then I resorted to a display of stupidity. I did not talk, and looked, if I looked at all, as if I did not understand. But he had seen glimpses of brightness in me the day before, and this ruse succeeded no better than the other. He even acted as if he admired me more as a breathing, sullen image than as a living, combative woman.

"My father, who watched us as he never had watched anything before but rising bubbles of gas or accumulating crystals, did not show the displeasure I feared, possibly because he saw that I was failing in all my endeavors; and when the meal over, he led the way to the parlor, he even smiled upon me in a not altogether unfriendly way. I felt a sinking of the heart when I saw that smile. Better to me were his frowns, for that smile told me that, love or no love, liking or no liking, I was to be made the bait to win this man's money for the uses of chemistry.

"Walking steadfastly into the parlor, I met the stranger's admiring eye.

"'You would not think,' I remarked, 'that my life at present was enclosed within these four walls.'

"It was the first sentence I had voluntarily addressed him, and it must have struck him as a very peculiar one.

"'I do not understand what you mean,' he returned, with that unctuous smile which to me was so detestable. 'Something interesting, I have no doubt.'

"'Very interesting,' I dryly rejoined. 'I have taken a vow never to leave this house, and I mean to keep it.'

"He stared at me now in some apprehension, and my heart gave a bound of delight. I had frightened him. He thought I was demented.

"My father, seeing his look of astonishment, but not knowing what I had said, here advanced and unconsciously made matters worse by remarking, with an effort at jocularity:

"'Don't mind what Hermione says; for a smart girl and a good one, she sometimes talks very peculiarly.'

"'I should think so,' my companion's manner seemed to assert, but he gave a sudden laugh, and made some observation which I scarcely heard in my fierce determination to end this matter at once.

"'Do you not think,' I persisted, 'that a woman who has doomed herself to perpetual seclusion has a right to be peculiar?'

"'A woman of such beauty possesses most any rights she chooses to assert,' was his somewhat lame reply. He had evidently received a shock, and was greatly embarrassed.

"'I laughed low to myself, but my father, comprehending as in a flash what I was attempting, turned livid and made me a threatening gesture.'

"'I fear,' said he, 'that you will have to excuse my daughter for to-night. The misfortune which has befallen her has soured her temper, and this is not one of her amiable days.'

"I made a curtsey deep as my disdain. 'I leave you to the enjoyment of your criticisms,' I exclaimed, and fled from the room in a flutter of mingled satisfaction and fear.

"For though I had saved myself from any possible persecution on the part of Mr. Harding, I had done it at the cost of any possible reconciliation between my father and myself. And I was not yet so hardened that I could contemplate years of such life as I was then living without a pang of dread. Alas! if I had known what I was indeed preparing for myself, and how much worse a future dwelt in his mind than any I had contemplated!

"Emma, who had been a silent and unobtrusive witness to what had occurred, soon followed me to my room.

"'What have you done?' she asked. 'Why speak so to a stranger?'

"'Father wants me to like him; father wants me to accept his attentions, and I detest him. I abhor his very presence in the house.'

"'But— —'

"'I know he has only been here but twice; but that is enough, Emma; he shall not come here again with any idea that he will receive the least welcome from me.'

"'Is he a person known to father? Is he— —'

"'Rich? Oh, yes; he is rich. That is why father thinks him an eligible son-in-law. His thousands would raise the threatened discovery into a fact.'

"'I see. I pity you, Hermione. It is hard to disappoint a father in his dearest hopes.'

"I stared at her in sudden fury.

"'Is that what you are thinking of?' I demanded, with reckless impetuosity. 'After all the cruel disappointment he has inflicted upon me— —'

"But Emma had slipped from the room. She had no words now with which to meet my gusts of temper.

"A visit from my father came next. Though strong in my resolve not to be shaken, I secretly quaked at the cold, cruel determination in his face. A man after all is so much more unrelenting than a woman.

"'Hermione,' he cried, 'you have disobeyed me. You have insulted my guest, and you have shaken the hopes which I thought I had a right to form, being your father and the author of your being. I said if you did this you should suffer, but I mean to give you one more chance. Mr. Harding was startled rather than alienated. If you show yourself in future the amiable and sensible woman which you can be, he will forget this foolish ebullition and make you the offer his passion inspires. This would mean worldly prosperity, social consideration, and everything else which a reasonable woman, even if she has been disappointed in love, could require. While for me—you cannot know what it would be for me, for you have no capability for appreciating the noble study to which I am devoted.'

"'No,' I said, hard and cold as adamant, 'I have no appreciation for a study which, like another Moloch, demands, not only the sacrifice of the self-respect, but even the lives of your unhappy children.'

"'You rave,' was his harsh reply. 'I offer you all the pleasures of life, and you call it immolation. Is not Mr. Harding as much of a gentleman as Dr. Sellick? Do I ask you to accept the attentions of a boor or a scape-grace? He is called a very honorable man by those who know him, and if you were ten times handsomer than you are, ten times more amiable, and had no defect calculated to diminish the regard of most men, you would still be scarcely worthy to bear the name of so wealthy, honorable, and highly esteemed a young man.'

"'Father, father!' I exclaimed, scarcely able to bear from him this allusion to my misfortune.

"'Why he has taken such a sudden, and, if I may say it, violent fancy to you, I find it hard to understand myself. But he has done this, and he has not scrupled to tell me so, and to intimate that he would like the opportunity of cultivating your good graces. Will you, then—I ask it for the last time—extend him a welcome, or must I see my hopes vanish, and with them a life too feeble to survive the disappointment which their loss must occasion.'

"'I cannot give any sort of welcome to this man,' I returned. 'If I did, I would be doing him a wrong, as well as you and myself. I dislike him, father, more than I can make you understand. His presence is worse than death to me; I would rather go to my coffin than to his arms. But if I liked him, if he were the beau-ideal of my dreams, could I break the vow I made one day in your presence? This man is not Dr. Sellick; do not then seek to make me forget the oath of isolation I have taken.'

"'Fool! fool!' was my father's furious retort. 'I know he is not Dr. Sellick. If he were I should not have his cause to plead to *you*.'

"How nearly his secret came out in his rage. 'If I could make you understand; make you see——'

"'You make me see that I am giving you a great and bitter disappointment,' I broke in. 'But it only equalizes matters; you have given me one.'

"He bounded to my side; he seized my arm and shook it.

"'Drop that foolish talk,' he cried. 'I will hear no more of it, nor of your staying in the house on that account or any other. You will go out to-morrow. You will go out with Mr. Harding. You will——'

"'Father,' I put in, chill as ice, 'do you expect to carry me out in your arms?'

"He fell back; he was a small man, my father, and I, as you know, am large for a woman.

"'You vixen!' he muttered, 'curses on the day when you were born!'

"'That curse has been already pronounced,' I muttered.

"He stood still, he made no answer, he seemed to be gathering himself together for a final appeal. Had he looked at me a little longer; had he shown any sympathy for my position, any appreciation for my wrongs, or any compunction for the share he had taken in them, I might have shown myself to have possessed some womanly softness and latent gentleness. But instead of that he took on in those few frightful moments such a look of cold, calculating hate that I was at once steeled and appalled. I hardly knew what he said when he cried at last:

"'Once! twice! thrice! Will you do what I desire, Hermione?'

"I only knew he had asked something I could not grant, so I answered, with what calmness I could, in the old formula, now for some months gone into disuse, 'I will not,' and sank, weary with my own emotions, into a chair.

"He gave me one look—I shall never forget it,—and threw up his arms with what sounded like an imprecation.

"'Then your sin be upon your own head!' he cried, and without another word left the room.

"I was frightened; never had I seen such an expression on mortal face before. And this was my father; the man who had courted my mother; who had put the ring upon her finger at the altar; who had sat at her dying bed and smiled as she whispered: 'For a busy man, you have always been a good husband to me.' Was this or that the real man as he was? Had these depths been always hidden within him, or had I created them there by my hardness and disobedience? I will never know."

XXIV.
FATHER AND CHILD.

"Thenight which followed this day was a sleepless one for me. Yet how I dreaded the morning! How I shrank from the first sight of my father's face! Had Auntie Lovell been with us I should have prevailed upon her to have gone to him and tried to smooth the way to some sort of reconciliation between us, but she was in Chicago, and I was not yet upon such terms with Emma that I could bear to make of her a go-between. I preferred to meet him without apology, and by dutifulness in all other respects make him forget in time my failure to oblige him in one. *I had made up my mind to go out of the house that day, though not with Mr. Harding.*

"But sometimes it seems as if Providence stepped in our way when we try to recover from any false position into which we have been betrayed by the heat and stress of our own passions. When I tried to rise I found myself ill, and for several days after that I knew little and cared less where I was, or what my future was like to be. When I was well enough to get up and go about my duties again, I found the house and my father in very much the same condition as they were before the fatal appearance of Mr. Harding. No look from his eye revealed that any great change had taken place in his attitude towards me, and after learning that Mr. Harding had come once since my illness, been closeted with my father for some time, and had then gone away with a rather formal and hard good-by to the anxious Emma, I began to feel that my fears had been part of the delirium of the fever which had afterwards set in, and that I was alarming myself and softening my heart more than was necessary.

"The consequence was that I did not go out that afternoon, nor the next morning, nor for a week after, though I was always saying to myself that I would surprise them yet by a sudden dash out of the house when they showed, or rather my father showed, any such relenting in his studied attitude of indifference as would make such an action on the part of one constituted like myself, possible.

"But he was thinking of anything else but relenting, and even I began to see in a few days that something portentous lay behind the apparent apathy of his manner. He worked as he had of old, or rather he shut himself up in his laboratory from morning until night, but when he did appear, there was something new in his manner that deeply troubled me. I began to shrink at the sound of his step, and more than once went without a meal rather than meet the cold glance of his eye.

"Emma, who seemed to have little idea of what I suffered and of what I dreaded (what did I dread? I hardly knew) used to talk to me sometimes of our father's failing health; but I either hushed her or sat like a stone, I was in such a state of shuddering horror. I remember one day as I stole past the laboratory door, I beheld her with her arms round his neck, and the sight filled me with tumult, but whether it was one of longing or repugnance, or a mixture of both, I can hardly tell. But I know it was with difficulty I repressed a cry of grief, and that when I found myself alone my limbs were shaking under me like those of one stricken with ague. At last there came a day when father was no longer to be seen at the table. He ordered his meals brought to the laboratory, but denied being sick. I stared at Emma, who delivered this message, and asked her what she thought of it.

"'That he *is* ill,' she declared.

"Two weeks later my father called me into his presence. I went in fear and trembling. He was standing by his desk in the laboratory, and I could not repress a start of surprise when I saw the change which had taken place in him. But I said nothing, only stood near the doorway and waited for what he had to say.

"'Look at me,' he commanded. 'I am standing to-day; to-morrow I shall be sitting. I wish you to watch your work; now go.'

"I turned, so shaken by his look and terrible wanness that I could hardly stand. But at the door I paused and cried in irrepressible terror:

"'You are ill; let me send for a doctor. I cannot see you dying thus before my eyes.'

"'You cannot?' With what a grim chuckle he uttered the words. 'We will see what you can bear.' Then as my eyes opened in terror, and I seemed about to flee, he cried, 'No doctor, do you hear? I will see none. And mark me, no talking about what goes on in this room, if you do not wish my curse.'

"Aghast, I rushed from that unhallowed door. What did his words mean? What was his purpose? Upon what precipice of horror was I stumbling?

"The next day he summoned me again. I felt too weak to go, but I dared not disobey. I opened his door with a shaking hand, and found him sitting, as he had promised, in an old arm-chair that had been his mother's.

"'Do I look any better?' he asked.

"I shook my head. He was evidently much worse.

"'The poison of disobedience works slowly, but it works sure,' he cried.

"I threw up my arms with a shriek.

"He seemed to love the sound.

"'You do not enjoy the fruits of your actions,' said he. 'You love your old father so dearly.'

"I held out my hands; I entreated; I implored.

"'Do not—do not look on me like this. Some dreadful thought is in your mind—some dreadful revenge. Do not cherish it; do not make my already ruined life a worse torture to me. Let me have help, let me send for a doctor— —'

"But his sternly lifted finger was already pointing at the door.

"'You have stayed too long,' he muttered. 'Next time you will barely look in, and leave without a word.'

"I crouched, he cowed me so, and then fled, this time to find Emma, Doris, some one.

"They were both huddled in the hall below. They had heard our voices and were terrified at the sound.

"'Don't you think he is very ill?' asked Emma. 'Don't you think we ought to have the doctor come, in spite of his commands to the contrary?'

"'Yes,' I gasped, 'and quickly, or we will feel like murderers.'

"'Dr. Dudgeon is a big know-nothing,' cried Doris.

"'But he is a doctor,' I said. And Doris went for him at once.

"When he came Emma undertook to take him to the laboratory; I did not dare. I sat on the stairs and listened, shaking in every limb. What was going on in that room? What was my father saying? What was the doctor deciding? When the door opened at last I was almost unconscious. The sound of the doctor's voice, always loud, struck upon my ears like thunder, but I could not distinguish his words. Not till he had come half-way down the stairs did I begin to understand them, and then I heard:

"'A case of overwork! He will be better in a day or two. Send for me if he seems any worse.'

"Overwork! that clay-white cheek! those dry and burning lips! the eyes hollowed out as if death were already making a skeleton of him! I seized the doctor's hand as he went by.

"'Are you sure that is all?' I cried.

"He gave me a pompous stare. 'I do not often repeat myself,' said he, and went haughtily out without another word.

"Emma, standing at the top of the stairs, came down as the door closed behind him.

"'Father was not so angry as I feared he would be. He smiled at the doctor and seemed glad to see him. He even roused himself up to talk, and for a few minutes did not look so ill as he really is.'

"'Did the doctor leave medicine?' I asked.

"'Oh, yes, plenty; powder and pills.'

"'Where is it?'

"'On father's desk. He says he will take it regularly. He would not let me give it to him.'

"I reeled; everything seemed turning round with me.

"'Watch him,' I cried, 'watch——' and could say no more. Unconsciousness had come to relieve me.

"It was dark when I came to myself. I was lying on my own bed, and by the dim light burning on a small table near by I saw the form of Doris bending over me. Starting up, I caught her by the arm.

"'What is going on?' I cried.

"Rude noises were in the house. A sound of breaking glass.

"'It comes from the laboratory,' she exclaimed, and rushed from the room.

"I rose and had barely strength enough to follow her. When we reached the laboratory door Emma was already there. A light was burning at one end of the long and dismal room, and amid the weird shadows that it cast we saw our father in a loose gown he often wore when at work, standing over his table with lifted fist. It was bleeding; he had just brought it down upon a favorite collection of tubes.

"'Ah!' he cried, tottering and seizing the table to steady himself; 'you have come to see the end of my famous discovery. Here it is; look!' And his fist came down again upon a jar containing the work of months.

"The smash that followed seemed to echo in my brain. I rushed forward, but was stopped by his look.

"'Another result of your obduracy,' he cried, and sank back fainting upon the hard floor.

"I let Emma and Doris lift him. What place had I at his side?

"'Shall I go for the doctor again?' inquired Doris as she came to my room a half-hour later.

"'Does he seem worse?' I asked.

"'No; but he looks dreadfully. Ever since we got him on the lounge—he would not leave the laboratory—he has lain in one position, his eye upon those broken pieces of glass. He would not even let me wipe up the red liquid that was in them, and it drips from table to floor in a way to make your blood run cold.'

"'Can I see him,' I asked, 'without his seeing me?'

"'Yes,' said she, 'if you come very carefully; his head is towards the door.'

"I did as she bade, and crept towards the open door. As I reached it he was speaking low to himself.

"'Drop by drop,' he was saying, 'just as if it were my life-blood that was dripping from the table to the floor.'

"It was a terrible thing to hear, for *me* to hear, and I shrank back. But soon a certain sense of duty drove me forward again, and I leaned across the threshold, peering at his rigid and attenuated figure lying just where he could watch the destruction of all his hopes. I could not see his face, but his attitude was eloquent, and I felt a pang strike through all my horror at the sight of a grief the death of both his children could not have occasioned him.

"Suddenly he bounded up.

"'Curse her!' he began, in a frenzy; but instantly seemed to bethink himself, for he sank back very meekly as Emma stooped over him and Doris rushed to his side. 'Excuse me,' said he; 'I fear I am not just in my right mind.'

"They thought so too, and in a few minutes Doris stole out after the doctor, but I knew whatever delirium he had sprang from his hate of me, and was awed into a shrinking inactivity which Emma excused while only partially understanding.

"The doctor came and this time I stood watching. My father, who had not expected this interference, showed anger at first, but soon settled back into a half-jocular, half-indifferent endurance of the interloper, which tended to impress the latter, and did succeed in doing so, with the folly of those who thought he was sick enough to rouse a doctor up at midnight. Few questions brought few replies, and the irritated physician left us with something like a rebuke. He however said he would come again in the morning, as there was a fitfulness in my father's pulse which he did not like.

"But before the doctor appeared that morning father had called me for the third and last time to his side.

"'I wish to see my eldest daughter alone,' he declared, as Emma lingered and Doris hovered about the open door. They at once went out. 'Now shut the door,' said he, as their footsteps were heard descending the stairs.

"I did as I was bid, though I felt as if I were shutting myself in with some horrid doom.

"'Now come in front of me,' he commanded, 'I want to look at you. I have just five minutes left in which to do it.'

"'Five minutes!' I repeated hoarsely, creeping round with tottering and yet more tottering steps to where he pointed.

"'Yes; the poison has done its work at last. At eight o'clock I shall be dead.'

"'Poison!' I shrieked, but in so choked a tone the word sounded like a smothered whisper.

"But he was alarmed by it for all that.

"'Do not tell the world,' he cried. 'It is enough that you know it. Are you pleased that you have driven your father to self-destruction? Will it make your life in this house, in which you have vowed to remain, any happier? I told you that your sin should be on your head; and it will be. For, listen to me: now in this last dreadful hour, I command you, heartless and disobedient one, to keep that vow. By this awful death, by the despair which has driven me to it, beware of leaving these doors. In your anger you swore to remain within these walls; in your remorse see that you keep that oath. Not for love, not for hatred, dare to cross the threshold, or I will denounce you in the grave where I shall be gone, and my curse shall be upon you.'

"He had risen in his passion as he uttered these words, but he sank back as he finished, and I thought he was dead. Terrified, crushed, I sank upon my knees, having no words with which to plead for the mercy for which I now longed. The next minute a horrible groan burst upon my ear.

"'It eats—it burns into my vitals. The suffering has come,—the suffering which I have often noted with unconcern in the animals upon which I tested it. I cannot bear it; I had rather live. Get me the antidote; there, there, in the long narrow drawer in the cabinet by the wall. Not there, not there!' he shrieked, as I stumbled over the floor, which seemed to rise in waves beneath my feet. 'The other cabinet, the other drawer; *you are where the poison is.*'

"I halted; weights seemed to be upon my feet; I could not move. He was writhing in agony on the floor; he no longer seemed to know where I stood.

"'Open it—the drawer,' he cried. 'Bring me what is in it.'

"I reached out my hand; heaven and earth seemed to stand still; red lights danced before my eyes; I drew out the drawer.

"'Quick, quick, the powder!' he moaned; 'fetch it!'

"I was staring at him, but my hand groped in the drawer. I felt a little packet of powder; I took it and crossed the room. As soon as I was near him he stretched out his hand and grasped it. I saw him empty it into his mouth; at the same instant his eyes fixed themselves in horror on the drawer I had left open behind me, the drawer in which the poison was kept.

"'Curse you for a——' He never said what. With this broken imprecation upon his lips, he sank back upon the floor, dead."

XXV.
EDGAR AND FRANK.

Frank, who had been reading these words as if swept along by a torrent, started to his feet with a hoarse cry, as he reached this point. He could not believe his eyes, he could not believe his understanding. He shrank from the paper that contained the deadly revelation, as though a snake had suddenly uncoiled itself from amid the sheets. With hair slowly rising on his forehead, he stared and stared, hoping wildly, hoping against hope, to see other words start from the sheet, and blot out of existence the ones that had in an instant made his love a horror, his life a desert.

But no, Heaven works no such miracle, even in sight of such an agony as his; and the words met his gaze relentlessly till his misery was more than he could endure, and he rushed from the room like a madman.

Edgar, who was busy over some medical treatise, rose rapidly as he heard the unsteady footsteps of his friend.

"What is the matter?" he cried, as Frank came stumbling into his presence. "You look— —"

"Never mind how I look; comfort me, Edgar, comfort me!" and in his anguish he burst into irrepressible sobs "Hermione is— —" He could not say what, but drew his friend after him to the room where the letter lay, and pointed to the few ghastly lines which had undone him. "Read those," he panted. "She had suffered; she was not herself, but, oh— —" He broke down again, and did not try to speak further till Edgar had read the hideous confession contained in those closing lines, and some of the revelations which had led up to it. Then he said: "Do not speak to me yet; let me bear the horror alone. I loved her so; ah, I did love her!"

Edgar, who had turned very pale, was considerate enough to respect this grief, and silently wait for Frank to regain sufficient composure to talk with him. This was not soon, but when the moment came, Edgar showed that his heart beat truly under all his apparent indifference. He did not say, "I bade you beware"; he merely took his friend's hand and wrung it. Frank, who was almost overwhelmed with shame and sorrow, muttered some words of acknowledgment.

"I must get out of the town," said he. "I feel as if the very atmosphere here would choke me."

Here came again the long, doleful drone of the foghorn. "How like a groan that is," said he. "An evil day it was for me when I first came within its foreboding sound."

"We will say that when all is over," ventured Edgar, but in no very hopeful tones. "You should not have shown me these words, Frank; the wonder is that she was willing to show them to you."

"She could not otherwise get rid of my importunities. I would take no hint, and so she tells me the truth."

"That shows nobleness," remarked Edgar. "She has some virtues which may excuse you to yourself for the weakness you have shown in her regard."

"I dare not think of it," said Frank. "I dare not think of her again. Yet to leave her when she is suffering so! Is not that almost as cruel a fate as to learn that she is so unworthy?"

"I would you had never come here!" exclaimed Edgar, with unwonted fervency.

"There are more words," observed Frank, "but I cannot read them. "Words of sorrow and remorse, no doubt, but what do they avail? The fact remains that she gave her father in his agony another dose of the poison that was killing him, instead of the antidote for which he prayed."

"Yes," said Edgar, "only I feel bound to say that no antidote would have saved him then. I know the poison and I know the antidote; we have tested them together often."

Frank shuddered.

"He had the heart of a demon," declared Edgar, "to plan and carry out such a revenge, even upon a daughter who had so grievously disappointed him. I can hardly believe the tale, only that I have learned that one may believe anything of human nature."

"She—she did not kill him, then?"

"No, but her guilt is as great as if she had, for she must have had the momentary instinct of murder."

"O Hermione, Hermione! so beautiful and so unhappy!"

"A momentary instinct, which she is expiating fearfully. No wonder she does not leave the house. No wonder that her face looks like a tragic mask."

"No one seems to have suspected her guilt, or even his. We have never heard any whispers about poison."

"Dudgeon is a conceited fool. Having once said overwork, he would stick to overwork. Besides that poison is very subtle; I would have difficulty in detecting its workings myself."

"And this is the tragedy of that home! Oh, how much worse, how much more fearful than any I have attributed to it!"

The Doctor sighed.

"What has not Emma had to bear," he said.

"Emma!" Frank unconsciously roused himself. "If I remember rightly, Hermione has said that Emma did not know all her trouble."

"Thank God! May she never be enlightened."

"Edgar," whispered Frank, "I do not think I can let you read all that letter, though it tells much you ought to know. I have yet some consideration—for—for Hermione—" (How hard the word came from lips which once uttered it with so much pride!)—"and she never expected any other eyes than mine to rest upon these revelations of her heart of hearts. But one thing I must tell you in justice to yourself and the girl upon whom no shadow rests but that of a most loyal devotion to a most wretched sister. Not from her heart did the refusal come which blighted your hopes and made you cynical towards women. There were reasons she could not communicate, reasons she could not even dwell upon herself, why she felt forced to dismiss you, and in the seemingly heartless way she did."

"I am willing to believe it," said Edgar.

"Emma is a pure and beautiful spirit," observed Frank, and gave himself up to grief for her who was not, and yet who commanded his pity for her sufferings and possibly for her provocations.

Edgar now had enough of his own to think of, and if Frank had been less absorbed in his own trouble he might have observed with what longing eyes his friend turned every now and then towards the sheets which contained so much of Emma's history as well as her sister's. Finally he spoke:

"Why does Emma remain in the house to which the father only condemned her sister?"

"Because she once vowed to share that sister's fate, whatever it might be."

"Her love for her sister is then greater than any other passion she may have had."

"I don't know; there were other motives beside love to influence her," explained Frank, and said no more.

Edgar sank again into silence. It was Frank who spoke next.

"Do you think"—He paused and moistened his lips—"Have you doubted what our duty is about this matter?"

"To leave the girl—you said it yourself. Have you any other idea, Frank?"

"No, no; that is not what I mean," stammered Etheridge. "I mean about—about—the father's death. Should the world know? Is it a matter for the—for the police?"

"No," cried Edgar, aghast. "Mr. Cavanagh evidently killed himself. It is a dreadful thing to know, but I do not see why we need make it public."

Frank drew a long breath.

"I feared," he said,—"I did not know but you would think my duty would lie in—in——"

"Don't speak of it," exclaimed Edgar. "If you do not wish to finish reading her confession, put it up. Here is a drawer, in which you can safely lock it."

Frank, recoiling from the touch of those papers which had made such a havoc with his life, motioned to Edgar to do what he would with them.

"Are you not going to write—to answer this in some way?" asked Edgar.

"Thank God she has not made that necessary. She wrote somewhere, in the beginning, I think, that, if I felt the terror of her words too deeply, I was to pass by her house on the other side of the street at an early hour in the morning. Did she dream that I could do anything else?"

Edgar closed the drawer in which he had hidden her letter, locked it, and laid the key down on the table beside Frank.

Frank did not observe the action; he had risen to his feet, and in another moment had left the room. He had reached the point of feeling the need of air and a wider space in which to breathe. As he stepped into the street, he turned in a contrary direction to that in which he had been wont to walk. Had he not done this; had he gone southward, as usual, he might have seen the sly and crouching figure which was drawn up on that side of the house, peering into the room he had just left through the narrow opening made by an imperfectly lowered shade.

BOOK III.
UNCLE AND NIECE.

XXVI.
THE WHITE POWDER.

It was nine o'clock in the morning, and Hermione stood in the laboratory window overlooking the street. Pale from loss of sleep and exhausted with the fever of anxiety which had consumed her ever since she had despatched her letter to Mr. Etheridge, she looked little able to cope with any disappointment which might be in store for her. But as she leaned there watching for Frank, it was evident from her whole bearing that she was moved by a fearful hope rather than by an overmastering dread; perhaps because she had such confidence in his devotion; perhaps because there was such vitality in her own love.

Her manner was that of one who thinks himself alone, and yet she was not alone. At the other end of the long and dismal apartment glided the sly figure of Huckins. No longer shabby and unkempt, but dressed with a neatness which would have made his sister Cynthia stare in amazement if she could have risen from her grave to see him, he flitted about with noiseless tread, listening to every sigh that escaped from his niece's lips, and marking, though he scarcely glanced her way, each turn of her head and each bend of her body, as if he were fully aware of her reasons for standing there, and the importance of the issues hanging upon the occurrences of the next fifteen minutes.

She may have known of his presence, and she may not. Her preoccupation was great, and her attention fixed not upon anything in the room, but upon the street without. Yet she may have felt the influence of that gliding Evil, moving, snake-like, at her back. If she did she gave no sign, and the moments came and went without any change in her eager attitude or any cessation in the ceaseless movements with which he beguiled his own anxiety and the devilish purposes which were slowly forming themselves in his selfish and wicked mind.

At length she gave a start, and leaned heavily forward. Huckins, who was expecting this proof of sudden interest, paused where he was, and surveyed her with undisguised eagerness in his baleful eyes, while the words "She sees him; he is coming" formed themselves upon his thin and quivering lips, though no sound disturbed the silence, and neither he nor she seemed to breathe.

And he was right. Frank was coming down the street, not gayly and with the buoyant step of a happy lover, but with head sunk upon his breast and eyes lowered to the ground. Will he lift them as he approaches the gate? Will he smile, as in the olden time—the olden time that was yesterday—and raise his hand towards the gate and swing it back and enter with that lightsome air of his at once protecting and joy-inspiring? He looks very serious now, and his steps falter; but surely, surely, his love is not going to fail him at the crisis; surely, surely, he who has overlooked so much will not be daunted by the little more with which she has tried his devotion; surely, surely— — But his eyes do not lift themselves. He is at the gate, but his hand is not raised to it, and the smile does not come. He is going by, not on the other side of the street, but going by, going by, which means— —

As the consciousness of what it did mean pierced her heart and soul, Hermione gave a great cry—she never knew how great a cry—and, staring like one demented after the beloved figure that in her disordered sight seemed to shrink and waver as it vanished, sank helpless upon the window sill, with her head falling forward, in a deadly faint.

Huckins, hearing that cry, slowly rubbed his hands together and smiled as the Dark One might smile at the sudden downfall of some doubtful soul. Then he passed softly to the door, and, shutting it carefully, came back and recommenced his restless pacings, but this time with an apparent purpose of investigation, for he opened and shut drawers, not quietly, but with a decided clatter, and peered here and there into bottles and jars, casting, as he did so, ready side-glances at the drooping figure from which the moans of a fatal despair were now slowly breaking.

When those moans became words, he stopped and listened, and this was what he heard come faltering from her lips:

"Twice! twice! Once when I felt myself strong and now when I feel myself weak. It is too much for a proud woman. I cannot bear it."

At this evidence of revolt and discouragement, Huckins' smile grew in its triumph. He seemed to glide nearer to her; yet he did not stir.

She saw nothing. If she had once recognized his presence, he was to her now as one blotted from existence. She was saying over and over to herself: "No hope! no hope! I am cursed! My father's hate reaches higher than my prayers. There is no escape; no love, no light. Solitude is before me; solitude forever. Believing this, I cannot live; indeed I cannot!"

As if this had been the word for which he was waiting, Huckins suddenly straightened up his lean figure and began himself to talk, not as she did, in wild and passionate tones, but in low, abstracted murmurs, as if he were too intent upon a certain discovery he had made to know or care whether there was or was not any one present to overhear his words.

And what did he say? what could he say at a moment like this? Listen and gauge the evil in the man, for it is deep as his avarice and relentless as his purpose to enjoy the riches which he considers his due. He is standing by a cabinet, the cabinet on the left of the room, and his hand is in a long and narrow drawer.

"What is this?" (Mark the surprise in his tone.) "A packet labelled *Poison*? This is a strange thing to find lying about in an open drawer. *Poison!* I wonder what use brother Cavanagh had for poison?"

He pauses; was it because he had heard a moan or cry break from the spot where Hermione crouched against the wall? No, there was silence there, a deep and awful silence, which ought to have made the flesh creep upon his bones, but which, instead, seemed to add a greater innocence to his musing tones.

"I suppose it was what was left after some old experiment. It is very dangerous stuff. I should not like to drop these few grains of white powder upon my tongue, unless I wanted to be rid of all my troubles. Guess I had better shake the paper out of the window, or those girls will come across it some day, and may see that word Poison and be moved by it. Life in this house hasn't many attractions."

Any sound now from that dim, distant corner? No, silence is there still; deadly silence. He smiles darkly, and speaks again; very low now, but oh, how clearly!

"But what business is it of mine? I find poison in this drawer, and I leave it where I find it, and shut the drawer. It may be wanted for rats, and it is always a mistake for old folks to meddle. But I should like to; I'd like to throw this same innocent-looking white powder out of the window; it makes *me* afraid to think of it lying shut up here in a drawer so easily opened— — My child! Hermione!" he suddenly shrieked, "what do you want?"

She was standing before him, a white and terrible figure.

"Nothing," came from her set lips, in a low and even tone; but she laid one hand upon the drawer he had half shut and with the other pointed to the door.

He shrank from her, appalled perhaps at his work; perhaps at her recognition of it.

"Don't," he feebly protested, shaking with terror, or was it with a hideous anxiety? "There is poison in that drawer; do not open it."

"Go for my sister," was the imperious command. "I have no use for you here, but for her I have."

"You won't open that drawer," he prayed, as he retreated before her eyes in frightened jerks and breathless pauses.

"I tell you I do not need you," she repeated, her hand still on the drawer, her form rigid, her face blue-white and drawn.

"I—I will bring Emma," he faltered, and shambled across the threshold, throwing back upon her a look she may have noted and may not, but which if she had understood, would certainly have made her pause. "I will go for Emma," he said again, closing the door behind him with a touch which seemed to make even that senseless wood fall away from him. Then he listened—listened instead of going for the gentle sister whose presence might have calmed the turbulent spirit he had just left. And as he listened his face gradually took on a satisfied look, till, at a certain sound from within, he allowed his hands the luxury of a final congratulatory rub, and then gliding from the place, went below.

Emma was standing in the parlor window, fixed in dismay at the sight of Frank's going by without word or look; but Huckins did not stop to give her the message with which he had been entrusted. Instead of that he passed into the kitchen, and not till he had crossed the floor and shambled out into the open air of the garden did he venture to turn and say to the watching Doris:

"I am afraid Miss Hermione is not quite well."

XXVII.
THE HAND OF HUCKINS.

Frank exhausted his courage in passing Hermione's door. When he heard the cry she gave, he stopped for a moment, then rushed hastily on, not knowing whither, and not caring, so long as he never saw the street or the house or the poplars again.

He intended, as much as he intended anything, to take the train for New York, but when he came sufficiently to himself to think of the hour, he found that he was in a wood quite remote from the station, and that both the morning and noon trains had long since passed.

It was not much of a disappointment. He was in that stage of misery in which everything seems blurred, and life and its duties too unreal for contemplation. He did not wish to act or even to think. The great solitude about him was more endurable than the sight of human faces, but I doubt if he would have been other than solitary anywhere, or seen aught but her countenance in any place where he might have been.

And what made this the more torturing to him was the fact that he always saw her with an accusing look on her face. Never with bowed forehead or in an attitude of shame, but with the straightforward aspect of one utterly grieved where she had expected consideration and forbearance. This he knew to be a freak of his fancy, for had he not her words to prove she had merited his condemnation? But fancy or not, it followed him, softening unconsciously his thought of her, though it never for an instant weakened his resolve not to see her again or exchange another word with one whose conscience was laden with so heavy a crime.

The wood in which he found himself wandering skirted the town towards the west, so that when, in the afternoon, hunger and weariness drove him back to the abodes of men, he had but to follow the beaten track which ran through it, to come out at the other end of the village from that by which he had entered.

The place where he emerged was near a dark pool at the base of the hill on which was perched the Baptist church.

As he saw this pool and caught a sight of the steeple towering above him in the summer sky, he felt himself grow suddenly frantic. Here she had stood with Emma, halting between life and death. Here she had been seized by her first temptation, and had been saved from it only to fall into another one immeasurably greater and more damning. Horrible, loathsome pool! why had it not swallowed her? Would it not have been better that it had? He dared to think so, and bent above its dismal depths with a fascination which in another moment made him recoil and dash away in horror towards the open spaces of the high-road.

Edgar had just come in from his round of visits when Frank appeared before him. Having supposed him to be in New York, he uttered a loud exclamation. Whereupon Frank exclaimed:

"I could not go. I seemed to be chained to this place. I have been wandering all day in the woods." And he sank into a chair exhausted, caring little whether Edgar noted or not his weary and dishevelled appearance.

"You look ill," observed the Doctor; "or perhaps you have not eaten; let me get you a cup of coffee."

Frank looked up but made no further sign.

"You will stay with me to-night," suggested Edgar.

"I am chained," repeated Frank, and that was all.

With a look of sincerest compassion the Doctor quietly left the room. He had his own griefs, but he could master them; beside, the angel of hope was already whispering sweet messages to his secret soul. But Frank's trouble was beyond alleviation, and it crushed him as his own had never done, possibly because in this case his pride was powerless to sustain him. When he came back, he found Frank seated at the desk poring over the fatal letter. He had found the key of the drawer lying where he had left it, and, using it under a sudden impulse, had opened the drawer and taken out the sheets he had vowed never to touch again.

Edgar paused when he saw the other's bended head and absorbed air, and though he was both annoyed and perplexed he said nothing, but set down the tray he had brought very near to Frank's elbow.

The young lawyer neither turned nor gave it any attention.

Edgar, with the wonted patience of a physician, sat down and waited for his friend to move. He would not interrupt him, but would simply be in readiness to hand the coffee when Frank turned. But he never handed him that cup of coffee, for suddenly, Frank, with a wild air and eyes fixed in a dazed stare upon the paper, started to his feet, and uttering a cry, began turning over the two or three sheets he was reading, as if he had made some almost incomprehensible discovery.

"Edgar, Edgar," he hurriedly gasped, "read these over for me; I cannot see the words; there is something different here; we have made a mistake! Oh, what has happened! my head is all in a whirl."

He sank back in his chair. Edgar, rushing forward, seized the half dozen sheets offered him and glanced eagerly over them.

"I see no difference," he cried; but as he went on, driven by Frank's expectant eye, he gave a surprised start also, and turning back the pages, read them again and again, crying at last:

"We must have overlooked one of these sheets. We read her letter without this page. What a mischance! for with these words left in it is no longer a confession we have before us, but a narrative. Frank, Frank, we have wronged the girl. She has no crime to bemoan, only a misery to relate."

"Read it aloud," broke from Frank's lips. "Let me hear it from your mouth. How could we have overlooked such a page? Oh, my poor girl! my poor girl!"

Edgar, beginning back a page or two from the one which had before escaped their attention, read as follows. The portion marked by brackets is the one that was new to both their eyes:

"But before the doctor appeared that morning father had called me for the third and last time to his side.

"'I wish to see my eldest daughter alone,' he declared, as Emma lingered and Doris hovered about the open door. They at once went out. 'Now shut the door,' said he, as their footsteps were heard descending the stairs.

"I did as I was bid, though I felt as if I were shutting myself in with some horrid doom.

"'Now come in front of me,' he commanded. 'I want to look at you; I have just five minutes left in which to do it.'

"'Five minutes!' I repeated hoarsely, creeping round with tottering and yet more tottering steps to where he pointed.

"'Yes; the poison has done its work at last. At eight o'clock I shall be dead.'

"'Poison!' I shrieked, but in so choked a tone the word sounded like a smothered whisper.

"But he was alarmed by it for all that.

"'Do not tell the world,' he cried. 'It is enough that you know it. Are you pleased that you have driven your father to self-destruction? Will it make your life in this house, in which you have vowed to remain, any happier? I told you that your sin should be on your head, and it will be. For, listen to me: now in this last dreadful hour, I command you, heartless and disobedient one, to keep that vow. By this awful death, by the despair which has driven me to it, beware of leaving these doors. In your anger you swore to remain within these walls; in your remorse see that you keep that oath. Not for love, not for hatred, dare to cross the threshold, or I will denounce you in the grave where I shall be gone, and my curse shall be upon you.'

"He had risen in his passion as he uttered these words, but he sank back as he finished, and I thought he was dead.

"Terrified, crushed, I sank upon my knees, having no words with which to plead for the mercy for which I now longed. The next minute a horrible groan burst upon my ear.

"'It eats—it burns into my vitals. The suffering has come,— the suffering which I have often noted with unconcern in the animals upon which I had tested it. I cannot bear it; I had rather live. Get me the antidote; there, there in the long, narrow drawer in the cabinet by the wall! Not there, not there!' he shrieked, as I stumbled over the floor, which seemed to rise in waves beneath my feet. 'The other cabinet, the other drawer; *you are where the poison is.*'

"I halted; weights seemed to be upon my feet; I could not move. He was writhing in agony on the floor; he no longer seemed to know where I stood.

"'The antidote!' he moaned, 'the antidote!' I burst the bonds which held me, and leaving open the drawer which I had half pulled out in my eagerness to relieve him, I rushed across the room to the cabinet he had pointed out.

"'The long drawer,' he murmured, 'the one like the other. Pull it hard; it is not locked!'

"I tried to do as he commanded, but my hand slid helplessly from drawer to drawer. I could hardly see. He moaned and shrieked again.

"'The long one, I say, the long one!'

"As he spoke my hand touched it.

"'I have it,' I panted forth.

"'Open it—the drawer,' he cried. 'Bring me what is in it.'

"I reached out my hand; heaven and earth seemed to stand still; red lights danced before my eyes; I drew out the drawer.

"'Quick, quick, the powder!' he moaned; 'fetch it!'

"I was staring at him, but my hand groped in the drawer. I felt a little packet of powder; I took it and crossed the room. As soon as I was near him he stretched out his hand and grasped it. I saw him empty it into his mouth; at the same instant his eyes fixed themselves in horror on the drawer I had left open behind me, the drawer in which the poison was kept.

"'Curse you for a — —' He never said what. With this broken imprecation upon his lips, he sank back upon the floor, dead."

"God, what a difference!" cried Edgar. But Frank, trembling from head to foot, reached out and took the sheets, and laying them on the desk before him, buried his face in them. When he looked up again, Edgar, for all his own relief, was startled by the change in him.

"Her vindication comes late," said he, "but I will go at once and explain— —"

"Wait; let us first understand how we both were led to make such a mistake. Could the leaves have stuck together?"

There were no signs of this having happened. Yet who could say that this was not the real explanation of the whole matter? The most curious feature of the occurrence was that just the missing of that one sheet should have so altered the sense of what they read. They did not know then or ever that this very fact had struck Huckins also in his stolen reading of the same, and that it had been his hand which had abstracted it and then again restored it when he thought the mutilated manuscript had done its work. They never knew this, as I say, but they thought the chance which had occurred to them a very strange one, and tried to lay it to their agitation at the time, or to any cause but the real one.

The riddle proving insolvable, they abandoned it, and Frank again rose. But Edgar drawing his attention to the few additional sheets which he had never read, he sat down again in eagerness to peruse them. Let us read them with him, for in them we shall find the Hermione of to-day, not the angry and imperious woman upon whom her father revenged himself by a death calculated to blot the sun from her skies and happiness from her heart forever.

"When Emma came to the room she discovered me kneeling, rigid and horror-stricken, above my father's outstretched form. She says that I met her eyes with mine, but that there was no look of life within them. Indeed, I was hardly alive, and have no remembrance of how I was taken from that room or what happened in the house for hours. When I did rouse, Emma was beside me. Her look was one of grief but not of horror, and I saw she had no idea of what had passed between my father and myself during the last few days. Dr. Dudgeon had told her that our father had died of heart-disease, and she believed him, and thought my terror was due to the suddenness of his end and the fact that I was alone with him at the time.

"She therefore smiled with a certain faint encouragement when I opened my eyes upon her face, but pushed me back with gentle hand when I tried to rise, saying:

"'All is well with father, Hermione,—so think only of yourself just now; I do not think you are able to get up.'

"I was only too happy not to make the effort. If only my eyes had never opened! If only I had sunk from unconsciousness into the perfect peace of death! But even that idea made me quake. *He* was *there*, and I had such a horror of him, that it seemed for a moment that I would rather live forever than to encounter him again, even in a world where the secrets of all hearts lie open.

"'Did not father forgive you?' murmured Emma, marking perhaps the expression of my face.

"I smiled a bitter smile.

"'Do not ever let us talk about father,' I prayed. 'He has condemned me to this house, and that will make me remember him sufficiently without words.'

"She rose horror-stricken.

"'O Hermione!' she murmured; 'O Hermione!' and hid her face in her hands and wept.

"But I lay silent, tearless.

"When the funeral procession passed out of the house without us, the people stared. But no thought of there being anything back of this seeming disrespect, save the caprice of two very whimsical girls, seemed to strike the mind of any one. The paper which had held the antidote I had long ago picked up from the laboratory floor; while the open drawer with the packet in it marked *Poison* had doubtless been shut by Doris on her first entrance into the room after his death. For I not only found it closed, but I never heard any one speak of it, or of any peculiar symptoms attending my father's death.

"But the arrow was in my heart for all that, and for weeks my life was little more than a nightmare. All the pride which had upheld me was gone. I felt myself a crushed woman. The pall which my father had thrown over me in his self-inflicted death, hung heavy and stifling about me. I breathed, but it seemed to be in gasps, and when exhausted nature gave way and I slept, it was to live over again in dreams those last fearful moments of his life, and hear, with even more distinctness than in my waking hours, the words of the final curse with which he sank to the floor.

"I had not deserved it—that I felt; but I suffered all the same, and suffered all the more that I could take no confidant into my troubles. Emma, with her broken life, had had disappointments enough without this revelation of a father's vindictiveness, and though it might have eased me for the moment to hear her words of sympathy, I knew that I should find it harder to face her day by day, if this ghost of horror once rose between us. No; the anguish was mine, and must be borne by me alone. So I crushed it down into my heart and was silent.

"Meantime the command which had been laid upon me by my father, never to leave the house, was weaving a chain about me I soon found it impossible to break. Had I immediately upon his death defied his will and rushed frenziedly out of the gate, I might have grown to feel it easy to walk the streets again in the face of a curse which should never have been laid upon me. But the custom of obeying his dying mandate soon got its hold upon me, and I could not overcome it. At the very thought of crossing the threshold I would tremble; and though when I looked at Emma heroically sharing my fate without knowing the reasons for my persistency, I would dream for a moment of breaking the spell those dying lips had laid upon me, I always found myself drawing back in terror, almost as if I had been caught by fleshless fingers.

"And so the weeks passed and we settled into the monotonous existence of an uninterrupted seclusion. What had been the expression of my self-will, became now a species of expiation. For though I had not deserved the awful burden which had been imposed upon me of a father's death and curse, I had deserved punishment, and this I now saw, and this I now endeavored to meet, with something like the meekness of repentance. I accepted my doom, and tried not to dwell so much upon my provocations as upon the temper with which I met them, and the hardness with which I strove to triumph over my disappointments. And in doing this I became less hard, preparing my heart, though I did not know it, for that new seed of love which fate was about to drop into it.

"Mr. Etheridge, I have told you all my story. If it strikes you with dismay and you shrink in your noble manhood from a woman whom, rightfully or wrongfully, is burdened with the weight of a father's death, do not try to overcome that shrinking or defy that dismay. We could never be happy if you did. Nothing but whole-souled love will satisfy me or help me to forget the shadows that bear so heavily upon my head. You say you love me, but your emotions upon reading this letter will prove to yourself what is the true strength and nature of your feelings. Let them, then, have their honest way. If they are in my favor I shall be the happiest girl alive, but if they lead you to go by on the other side of the street, then will I strive to bear this sorrow also, as one who has been much to blame for the evils which have befallen her."

That was all. As Frank folded the last sheet and put it and the rest quietly away in his pocket, Edgar saw, or thought he saw, that happier hours were about to dawn for Hermione Cavanagh. It made him think of his own love and of the claims of the gentle Emma.

"Frank," said he, with the effort of a reticent man compelled at last to make an admission, "if you are going to the Cavanaghs, I think—I—will—go—with you."

Frank started and leaped forward warmly with outstretched hand. But before their two palms could meet, the door was violently opened and a messenger came panting in with the announcement:

"Dr. Sellick's wanted. Hermione Cavanagh is at the point of death."

XXVIII.
IN EXTREMITY.

Frank and Edgar were equally pale as they reached the Cavanagh house. No time had been lost on the way, and yet the moments had been long enough for them both to be the prey of the wildest conjectures. The messenger who had brought the startling news of Hermione's illness knew nothing concerning the matter beyond the fact that Doris, their servant, had called to him, as he was passing their house, to run for Dr. Sellick, as Miss Hermione was dying. They were therefore entirely in the dark as to what had happened, and entered the house, upon their arrival, like men for whom some terrible doom might be preparing.

The first person they encountered was Huckins. He was standing in the parlor window, rubbing his hands slowly together and smiling very softly to himself. But when he saw the two young men, he came forward with a cringing bow and an expression of hypocritical grief, which revived all Frank's distrust and antipathy.

"Oh, sir," he exclaimed to Frank, "you here? You should not have come; indeed you should not. Sad case," he added, turning to the Doctor; "very sad case, this which we have upstairs. I fear we are going to lose the dear young lady." And he wiped his half-shut eyes with his fine white handkerchief.

"Let me see her; where is she?" cried the Doctor, not stopping to look around him, though the place must have been full of the most suggestive associations.

"Doris will show you. She was in the laboratory when I saw her last. A dangerous place for a young lady who has been jilted by her lover!" And he turned a very twinkling eye on Frank.

"What do you mean?" cried Frank. "The laboratory! The place where—— O Edgar, go to her, go at once."

But Edgar was already half-way upstairs, at the top of which he was met by Doris.

"What is this?" he cried. "What has happened to Miss Cavanagh?"

"Come and see," she said. "O that she should go out of the house first in this way!"

Alarmed more by the woman's manner than her words, Dr. Sellick hurried forward and entered the open laboratory door almost without realizing that in another instant he would be in the presence of Emma. And when he did see her, and met the eyes he had not looked into since that night a year before when she listened to his vows with such a sweet and bashful timidity, he hardly felt the shock of the change observable in her, for the greater shock her sister's appearance inspired. For Hermione lay on that same old couch which had once held her father, ill to speechlessness, and though the Doctor did not know what had brought her to this condition, he began to suspect and doubt if he were in time to revive her.

"What has she taken?" he demanded. "Something, or she would not be as low as this without more warning."

Emma, quaking, put a little piece of paper in his hand.

"I found this in her pocket," she whispered. "It was only a little while ago. It is quite empty," said she, "or you would have had two patients."

He stared at her, hardly taking in her words. Then he leaped to the door.

"Frank," he cried, tossing down a slip of paper on which he had hastily written a word, "go with this to the druggist at once! Run, for moments are precious!"

They heard a shout in answer; then the noise of the front door opening and shutting, and the sound of rapidly departing steps.

"Thank God!" the young physician murmured, as he came back into the laboratory, "that I studied chemistry with Mr. Cavanagh, or I might not know just what antidote was required here."

"Look!" Emma whispered; "she moved, when you said the word *Frank*."

The Doctor leaned forward and took Emma's hand.

"If we can rouse her enough to make her speak, she will be saved. When did she take that powder?"

"I fear she took it this morning, shortly after—after nine o'clock; but she did not begin to grow seriously ill till an hour ago, when she suddenly threw up her arms and shrieked."

"And didn't you know; didn't you suspect——"

"No, for she said nothing. She only looked haggard and clung to me; clung as if she could not bear to have me move an inch away from her side."

"And how long has she been unconscious and in that clammy, cold sweat?"

"A little while; just before we sent for you. I—I hated to disturb you at first, but life is everything, and——"

He gave her one deep, reassuring look.

"Emma," he softly murmured, "if we save your sister, four hearts shall be happy. See if you can make her stir. Tell her that Frank is here, and wants to see her."

Emma, with a brightening countenance, leaned over and kissed Hermione's marble-like brow.

"Hermione," she cried, "Hermione! Frank wants you; he is tired of waiting. Come, dear; shall I not tell him you will come?"

A quiver at the word *Frank*, but that was all.

"It is Frank, dear; Frank!" Emma persisted. "Rouse up long enough just to see him. He loves you, Hermione."

Not even a quiver now. Dr. Sellick began to turn pale.

"Hermione, will you leave us now, just as you are going to be happy? Listen, listen to Emma. You know I have always told you the truth. Frank is here, ready to love you. Wake, darling; wake, dearest——"

There was no use. No marble could be more unresponsive. Dr. Sellick rushed in anguish to the door. But the step he heard there was that of Huckins, and it was Huckins' face he encountered at the head of the stairs.

"Is she dead?" cried that worthy, bending forward to look into the room. "I was afraid, *very* much afraid, you could not do any good, when I saw how cold she was, poor dear."

The Doctor, not hearing him, shouted out: "The antidote! the antidote! Why does not Frank come!"

At that instant Frank was heard below: "Am I in time?" he gasped. "Here it is; I ran all the way"; and he came rushing up the stairs just as Huckins slipped from the step where he was and fell against him.

"Oh," whimpered that old hypocrite, "I beg your pardon; I am so agitated!" But his agitation seemed to spring mainly from the fact that the antidote Frank brought was in powder and not in a bottle, which might have been broken in their encounter.

Dr. Sellick, who saw nothing but the packet Frank held, grasped the remedy and dashed back into the room. Frank followed and stood in anguished suspense within the open doorway. Huckins crouched and murmured to himself on the stair.

"Can we get her to take it? Is there hope?" murmured Emma.

No word came in reply; the Doctor was looking fixedly at his patient.

"Frank," he said solemnly, "come and take her hand in yours. Nothing else will ever make her unlock her lips."

Frank, reeling in his misery, entered and fell at her feet.

"Hermione," he endeavored to say, but the word would not come. Breaking into sobs he took her hand and laid his forehead upon it. Would that anguish of the beloved one arouse her? Dr. Sellick and Emma drew near together in their anxiety and watched. Suddenly a murmur escaped from the former, and he bent rapidly forward. The close-locked lips were parting, parting so slowly, so imperceptibly, that only a physician's eye could see it. Waiting till they were opened enough to show the pearly teeth, he stooped and whispered in Frank's ear. Instantly the almost overwhelmed lover, roused, saw this evidence of existing life, and in his frenzied relief imprinted one wild kiss upon the hand he held. It seemed to move her, to reach her heart, to stay the soul just hovering on the confines of life, for the lips parted further, the lids of the eyes trembled, and before the reaction came, Dr. Sellick had succeeded in giving her a few grains of the impalpable powder he was holding.

"It will either kill or restore her," said he. "In five minutes we shall know the result."

And when at the end of those five minutes they heard a soft sigh, they never thought, in their sudden joy and relief, to look for the sneaking figure trembling on the staircase, who, at this first sign of reviving life in one he thought dead, slid from his station and went creeping down the stairs, with baffled looks that would have frightened even Doris had she seen them.

XXIX.
IN THE POPLAR WALK.

Two days had passed. Hermione was sitting in the cheerful sitting-room with the choicest of flowers about her and the breeze from the open window fluttering gayly in her locks. She was weak yet, but there was promise of life in her slowly brightening eye, and from the language of the smile which now and then disturbed the lines of her proud lips, there was hope of happiness in the heart which but two short days before had turned from life in despair.

Yet it was not a perfect hope, or the smiles would have been deeper and more frequent. She had held a long talk with Frank, but he had not touched upon a certain vital question, perhaps because he felt she had not yet the strength to argue it. He was her lover and anticipated marrying her, but he had not said whether he expected her to disobey her father and leave her home. She felt that he must expect this; she also felt that he had the right to do so; but when she thought of yielding to his wishes, the old horror returned to her, and a suffocating feeling of fear, as if it would never be allowed. The dead have such a hold upon us. As the pleasure of living and the ecstasy of love began to make themselves felt again in her weakened frame, she could not refrain from asking herself by what right she contemplated taking up the joys of life, who had not only forfeited them by her attempt at suicide, but who had been cursed by a father and doomed by his will to perpetual imprisonment. Had he not said, "Let not hatred, let not *love*, lead you to leave these doors"? How then presume to think of it or dream that she could be happy with such remembrances as hers ever springing up to blight her life? She wished, oh! how she wished, that Frank would not ask her to leave her home. Yet she knew this was weakness, and that soon, at the next interview, perhaps, she would have to dash his hopes by speaking of her fears. And so Hermione was not perfectly happy.

Emma, on the contrary, was like a bird loosed from a cage. She sang, yes, sang as she flitted up and down the stairs, and once Hermione started and blushed with surprise as her voice in a merry peal of laughter came from the garden. Such a sound had not been heard in that house for a year; such a sound seemed an anomaly there. Yet how sweet it was, and how it seemed to lift the shadows.

There was another person who started as this unusual note of merriment disturbed the silence of the garden. It was Huckins, who was slowly walking up and down beneath the poplars. He was waiting for Doris, and this sound went through him like an arrow.

"Laughter," he muttered, shaking his trembling hands in menace towards her. "That is a sound I must crush. It speaks too much of hope, and hope means the loss to me of all for which I have schemed for years. Why didn't that poison work? Why did I let that doctor come? I might have locked the door against him and left them to hunt for the key. But I was afraid; that Etheridge is so ready to suspect me."

He turned and walked away from the house. He dreaded to hear that silvery sound again.

"If she had died, as I had every reason to suspect after such a dose, Emma would have followed her in a day. And then who could have kept me out of my property? Not Etheridge, for all his hatred and suspicion of me." He shook his hand again in menace and moved farther down the path.

As his small black figure disappeared up the walk Doris appeared at the kitchen door. She also looked cheerful, yet there was a shade of anxiety in her expression as she glanced up the walk.

"He says he is going away," she murmured. "The shock of Miss Hermione's illness was too much for him, poor man! and he does not seem to consider how lonesome I will be. If only he had asked me to go with him! But then I could not have left the young ladies; not while they stick to this old horror of a house. What is it, Miss Emma?"

"A four-leaved clover! one, two, *three* of them," cried her young mistress from the lawn at the side of the house. "We are in luck! Times are going to change for us all, I think."

"The best luck we can have is to quit this house forever," answered Doris, with a boldness unusual on her lips.

"Ah," returned Emma, with her spirits a little dashed, "I cannot say about that, but we will try and be happy in it."

"Happy in it!" repeated Doris, but this time to herself. "I can never be happy in it, now I have had my dreams of pleasure abroad." And she left the kitchen door and began her slow walk towards the end of the garden.

Arrived at the place where Huckins waited for her, she stopped.

"Good afternoon," said she. "Pleasant strolling under these poplars."

He grunted and shook his head slowly to and fro.

"Nothing is very pleasant here," said he. "I have stood it as long as I can. My nieces are good girls, but I have failed to make them see reason, and I must leave it now to these two lovers of theirs to do what they can."

"And do you think they will succeed? That the young ladies will be influenced by them to break up their old habits?"

This was what Huckins did think, and what was driving him to extremity, but he veiled his real feelings very successfully under a doleful shake of the head.

"I do not know," said he. "I fear not. The Cavanagh blood is very obstinate, very obstinate indeed."

"Do you mean," cried Doris, "that they won't leave the house to be married? That they will go on living here in spite of these two young gentlemen who seem to be so fond of them?"

"I do," said he, with every appearance of truth. "I don't think anything but fire will ever drive them out of this house."

It was quietly said, almost mournfully, but it caused Doris to give a sudden start. Looking at him intently, she repeated "Fire?" and seemed to quake at the word, even while she rolled it like a sweet morsel under her tongue.

He nodded, but did not further press the subject. He had caught her look from the corner of his eye, and did not think it worth while to change his attitude of innocence.

"I wish," he insinuated, "there was another marriage which could take place."

"Another marriage?" she simpered.

"I have too much money for one to spend," said he. "I wish I knew of a good woman to share it."

Doris, before whose eyes the most dazzling dreams of wealth and consequence at once flashed, drooped her stout figure and endeavored to look languishing.

"If it were not for my duty to the young ladies," sighed she.

"Yes, yes," said he, "you must never leave them."

She turned, she twisted, she tortured her hands in her endeavor to keep down the evidences of her desire and her anxiety.

"If—if this house should be blown down in a storm or—or a fire should consume it as you say, they would have to go elsewhere, have to marry these young men, have to be happy in spite of themselves."

"But what cyclones ever come here?" he asked, with his mockery of a smile. "Or where could a fire spring from in a house guarded by a Doris?"

She was trembling so she could not answer. "Come out here again at six o'clock," said she; "they will miss me if I stay too long now. Oh, sir, how I wish I could see those two poor loves happy again!"

"How I wish you could!" said he, and there was nothing in his tone for her ears but benevolence.

As Huckins crept from the garden-gate he ran against Frank, who was on his way to the station.

"Oh, sir," he exclaimed, cringing, "I am sure I beg your pardon. Going up to town, eh?"

"Yes, and I advise you to do the same," quoth the other, turning upon him sharply. "The Misses Cavanagh are not well enough at present to entertain visitors."

"You are no doubt right," returned Huckins with his meekest and most treacherous aspect. "It is odd now, isn't it, but I was just going to say that it was time I left them, much as I love the poor dears. They seem so happy now, and their prospects are so bright, eh?"

"I hope so; they have had trouble enough."

"Um, um, they will go to Flatbush, I suppose, and I—poor old outcast that I am—may rub my hands in poverty."

He looked so cringing, and yet so saturnine, that Frank was tempted to turn on his heel and leave him with his innuendoes unanswered. But his better spirit prevailing, he said, after a moment's pregnant silence:

"Yes; the young ladies will go to Flatbush, and the extent of the poverty you endure will depend upon your good behavior. I do not think either of your nieces would wish to see you starve."

"No, no, poor dears, they are very kind, and the least I can do is to leave them. Old age and misery are not fit companions for youth and hope, are they, Mr. Etheridge?"

"I have already intimated what I thought about that."

"So you have, so you have. You are such a lawyer, Mr. Etheridge, such an admirable lawyer!"

Frank, disgusted, attempted to walk on, but Huckins followed close after him.

"You do not like me," he said. "You think because I was violent once that I envy these sweet girls their rights. But you don't know me, Mr. Etheridge; you don't know my good heart. Since I have seen them I have felt very willing to give up my claims, they are such nice girls, and will be so kind to their poor old uncle."

Frank gave him a look as much as to say he would see about that, but he said nothing beyond a short "What train do you take?"

As Huckins had not thought seriously of taking any, he faltered for a moment and then blurted out:

"I shall get off at eight. I must say good-by to the young ladies, you know."

Frank, who did not recognize this *must*, looked at his watch and said:

"You have just a half hour to get the train with me; you had better take it."

Huckins, a little startled, looked doubtfully at the lawyer and hesitated. He did not wish to arouse his antagonism or to add to his suspicion; indeed it was necessary to allay both. He therefore, after a moment of silent contemplation of the severe and inscrutable face before him, broke into a short wheedling laugh, and saying, "I had no idea my company was so agreeable," promised to make what haste he could and catch the six o'clock train if possible.

But of course it was not possible. He had his second interview with Doris to hold, and after that was over there were the young ladies to see and impress with the disinterested state of his feelings. So that it was eight o'clock before he was ready to leave the town. But he did leave it at that hour, though it must have been with some intention of returning, or why did he carry away with him the key of the side-door of the old Cavanagh mansion?

XXX.
THE FINAL TERROR.

A week went by and Frank returned to Marston full of hope and definite intention. He had notified the Surrogate of the discovery of the real heirs to the Wakeham estate, and he had engaged workmen to put in order the old house in Flatbush against the arrival of the youthful claimants. All that there now remained to do was to induce the young ladies to leave the accursed walls within which they had so long immured themselves.

Edgar was awaiting him at the station, and together they walked up the street.

"Is it all right?" asked Frank. "Have you seen them daily?"

"Every day but to-day. You would hardly know Emma."

"And—and Hermione?"

"She shows her feelings less, but she is evidently happier than she has been for a year."

"And her health?"

"Is completely re-established."

"Have you kept your word? Have you talked of everything but what we propose to do?"

"I never break my word."

"And they? Have they said anything about leaving the house, or of going to Flatbush, or—or——"

"No; they have preserved as close a silence as ourselves. I imagine they do not think it proper to speak till we have spoken first."

"It may be; but I should have been pleased if you could have told me that Hermione had been seen walking outside the gate."

"You would?"

"Yes. I dread the struggle which I now see before me. It is the first step which costs, and I was in hopes she would have taken this in my absence."

"Yes, it would have prevented argument. But perhaps you will not have to argue. She may be merely waiting for the support of your arm."

"Whatever she is waiting for, she takes her first step down the street to-night. What a new world it will open before her!" And Frank unconsciously quickened his pace.

Edgar followed with a less impatient step but with fully as much determination. Pride was mingled with his love, and pride demanded that his future wife should not be held in any bonds forged by the obstinacy or the superstitious fears of a wayward sister.

They expected to see the girls at the windows, but they found the shutters closed and the curtains drawn. Indeed, the whole house had a funereal look which staggered Frank and made even Edgar stare in astonishment. "It was not like this yesterday," he declared. "Do they not expect you?"

"Yes, if my telegram was delivered."

"Let us see at once what is the matter."

It was Doris who came to the door. When her eyes fell upon the two young men, especially upon Frank, her whole countenance changed.

"Oh, Mr. Etheridge, is it you?" she cried. "I thought—I understood——" She did not say what, but her relieved manner made quite an impression on Frank, although it was, of course, impossible for him to suspect what a dangerous deed she had been contemplating at that very moment.

"Are the young ladies well?" he asked, in his haste to be relieved from his anxiety.

"Oh, yes, quite well," she admitted, somewhat mysteriously. "They are in there," she added, pointing to the parlor on the left.

Frank and Edgar looked at each other. They had always before this been received in the cheerful sitting-room.

"If something is not soon done to make Miss Hermione leave the house," Doris whispered passionately to Frank as she passed him, "there will be worse trouble here than there has ever been before."

"What do you mean?" he demanded, gliding swiftly after her and catching her by the arm just as she reached the back hall.

"Go in and see," said she, "and when you come out tell me what success you have had. For if you fail, then——"

"Then what——"

"Providence must interpose to help you."

She was looking straight at him, but that glance told him nothing. He thought her words strange and her conduct strange, but everything was strange in this house, and not having the key to her thoughts, the word *Providence* did not greatly startle him.

"I will see what I can do," said he, and returning to Edgar, who had remained standing by the parlor-door, he preceded him into that gloomy apartment.

The girls were both there, seated, as Frank perceived with a certain sinking of the heart, in the farthest and dimmest corner of this most forbidding place. Emma was looking towards them, but Hermione sat with downcast eyes and an air of discouragement about her Frank found it hard to behold unmoved.

"Hermione," said he, advancing into the middle of the room, "have you no welcome for me?"

Trembling with sudden feeling, she rose slowly to her feet; and her eyes lifted themselves painfully to his.

"Forgive me," she entreated, "I have had such a shock."

"Shock?"

"Yes. Look at my head! look at my hair!"

She bent forward; he hastened to her side and glanced at the rich locks towards which she pointed. As he did so, he recoiled in sudden awe and confusion. "What does it mean?" he asked. There were gray spots in those dusky tresses, spots which had never been there before.

"The fingers of a ghost have touched me," she whispered. "Wherever they fell, a mark has been left, and those marks sear my brain."

And then Frank noticed, with inward horror, that the spots were regular and ran in a distinct circle about her head.

"Hermione," he cried, "has your imagination carried you so far? Ghost? Do you believe in ghosts?"

"I believe in anything *now*," she murmured.

Frightened by her shudders and dazed by words he found it impossible to treat lightly with those mysterious marks before him, Frank turned for relief to Emma, who had risen also and stood a few steps behind them, with her face bent downward though the Doctor pressed close at her side.

"Do you understand her?" said Frank.

With an effort Emma moved forward. "It has frightened *me*," she whispered.

"What has? Let us hear all about it," demanded the Doctor, speaking for the first time.

Hermione gave him a wistful glance. "We are wretched girls," said she. "If you expected to relieve us from the curse, it is impossible; my father will not have it so."

"Your father!" quoth both of the young men, appalled not at the superstition thus evinced, but at the effect they saw it was likely to have upon her mind.

"Did you think you saw *him*?" added Frank. "When? Where?"

"In the laboratory—last night. I did not see him but I felt him; felt him strike my head with his fingers and drag me back. It was worse than death! I shall never get over it."

"Tell me the particulars; explain the whole matter to me. Imagination plays us ghastly tricks sometimes. Were you alone? Was it late?"

"Why didn't I come here this morning?" cried Edgar.

"It was long after midnight. I had received your letter and could not sleep, so I went into the laboratory, as we often do, to walk. It was the first time I had been there since I was ill, and it made me tremble to cross its hated threshold, but I had a question to decide, and I thought I ought to decide it there. But I trembled, as I say, and my hand shook so as I opened the door that I was more disturbed than astonished when my light went suddenly out, leaving me in total darkness. As I was by this time inside the laboratory I did not turn back to relight my candle, for the breeze I presently felt blowing through the room convinced me that this would be idle, and that till the window was shut, which let in such a stream of air, any attempt to bring a light into the room would be attended by the same results. I therefore moved rapidly across the room to the window, and was about to close it when I was suddenly arrested, and my arms were paralyzed by the feeling of a presence in the room behind my back. It was so vivid, so clear to my thoughts, that I seemed to see it, though I did not turn from the window. It was that of an old man—my father's,—and the menace with which the arms were lifted froze the blood in my veins.

"I had merited it; I had been near to breaking his command. I had meditated, if I had not decided, upon a sudden breaking away from the bondage he had imposed upon me; I had been on the point of daring his curse, and now it was to fall upon me. I felt the justice of his presence and fell, as if stricken, on my knees.

"The silence that followed may have been short, and it may have been long. I was almost unconscious from fright, remorse, and apprehension. But when I did rouse and did summon courage to turn and crawl from the room, I was conscious of the thing following me, and would have screamed, but that I had no voice. Suddenly I gave a rush; but the moment I started forward I felt those fingers fall upon my head and draw me back, and when I did escape it was with a force that carried me beyond the door and then laid me senseless on the floor; for I am no longer strong, Mr. Etheridge, and the hatred of the dead is worse than that of the living."

"You had a dream, a fearful dream, and these marks prove its vividness," declared Edgar. "You must not let your life be ruined by any such fantasies."

"Oh, that it had been a dream," moaned Hermione, "but it was more than that, as we can prove."

"Prove?"

"Come to the laboratory," cried Emma, suddenly. "There is something we want to show you there; something which I saw early this morning when I went in to close the window Hermione did not shut."

The young men, startled, did not wait for a second bidding; they followed the two girls immediately up-stairs.

"No one has been up these stairs but Doris and ourselves since you went down them a week ago," declared Hermione, as they entered the laboratory. "Now look at the lid of the mahogany desk—my father's desk."

They all went over to it, and Emma, pointing, seemed to ask what they thought of it. They did not know what to think, for there on its even surface they beheld words written with the point of a finger in the thick dust which covered it; and the words were legible and ran thus:

"In your anger you swore to remain within these walls; in your remorse see that you keep that oath. Not for love, not for hatred, dare to cross the threshold, or I will denounce you in the grave where I shall be gone, and my curse shall be upon you."

"My father's words to me in the dreadful hour of his death," whispered Hermione. "You may remember them, Mr. Etheridge; they were in the letter I wrote you."

Frank did remember them quite well, and for a moment he, like Edgar, stood a little dazed and shaken by a mystery he could not immediately fathom. But only for a moment. He was too vigorous, and his determination was too great, for him to be daunted long by even an appearance of the supernatural. So leaping forward, with a bright laugh, he drew his hand across the menacing words, and, effacing them at once, cried with a confident look at Hermione:

"So will I erase them from your heart if you only will let me, Hermione."

But she pointed with an awful look at her hair.

"Can you take these spots out also? Till you can, do not expect me to follow the beck of any hand which would lead me to defy my father's curse by leaving this house."

At this declaration both men turned pale, and unconsciously moved towards each other with a single thought. Had they looked at the door, they would have seen the inquisitive face of Doris disappear towards the staircase, with that air of determination which only ends in action. But they only saw each other and the purpose which was slowly developing in each of their minds.

"Come, Hermione," urged Frank, "this is no place for you. If you are going to stay in this house, I am going to stay with you; but this room is prohibited; you shall never enter it again."

He did not know how truly he spoke.

"Come," said Edgar, in his turn, to Emma, "we have had all the horrors we want; now let us go down-stairs and have a little cheerful talk in the sitting-room."

And Emma yielded; but Hermione hung back.

"I dread to go down," said she; "this seems the only place in which I can say farewell."

But Frank was holding out his hand, and she gradually gave in to its seduction and followed him down-stairs into the sitting-room, which was fast growing dusky.

"Now," said he, without heeding Emma and the Doctor, who had retreated to one of the farther windows, "if you wish to say farewell, I will listen to you; but before you speak, hear what I have to say. In a certain box which came with me this day from New York, and which is now at Mr. Lothrop's, there lies a gown of snowy satin made with enough lace to hide any deficiencies it may have in size or fit. With this gown is a veil snowy as itself, and on the veil there lies a wreath of orange blossoms, while under the whole are piled garments after garments, chosen with loving care by the only sister I have in the world, for the one woman in that world I wish to make my wife. If you love me, Hermione, if you think my devotion a true one, fly from this nest of hideous memories and superstitious fears, and in that place where you are already expected, put on these garments I have brought you, and with them a crown of love, joy, and hope, which will mean a farewell, not to me, but to the old life forever."

But Hermione, swaying aside from him, cried: "I cannot, I cannot; the rafters would fall if I tried to pass the door."

"Then," said Frank, growing in height and glowing with purpose, "they shall fall first on me." And seizing her in his arms, he raised her to his breast and fled with her out of the room and out of the house, her wild shriek of mingled terror and love trailing faintly after them till he stopped on the farther side of the gate, which softly closed behind them.

Emma, who was taken as much by surprise as her sister had been, looked at the empty place where Hermione had so lately stood, and cowered low, as if the terrible loneliness of the house, now *she* was gone, crushed upon her like a weight. Then she seized Edgar by the hand and ran out also; and Edgar pulled the great door to behind them, and the Cavanagh mansion, for the first time in a year, was a shell without inmates, a body without soul.

They found Hermione standing in the dark shadows cast here in the street by the overhanging trees. Frank's arm was about her and she looked both dazed and pleased.

When she saw Emma she started.

"Oh, it releases you too," she cried; "that is happiness. I did not like to see you suffer for my sins." Then she drooped a little, then she looked up, and a burden seemed to roll away from her heart. "The rafters did not fall," she murmured, "and you, Frank, will keep all spectres away from me, won't you? He can never reach me when I am by your side."

"Never, never," was the glad reply. And Frank began to draw her gently up the street. "It is but a step," said he, "to Mr. Lothrop's; no one will ever notice that you are without a hat."

"But— —"

"You are expected," he whispered. "You are never to go back into your old home again."

Again he did not know how truly he spoke.

"Emma, Emma," appealed Hermione, "shall I do this thing, without any preparation, any thought, anything but my love and gratitude to make it a true bridal?"

"Ah, Hermione, in making yourself happy, you make me so; therefore I am but a poor adviser."

"What, will you be married too, to-night, at the minister's house with me?"

"No, dear, but soon, very soon, as soon as you can give me a home to be married in."

"Then let us make her happy," cried Hermione. "It is the only reparation I can offer for all I have made her suffer."

XXXI.
AN EVENTFUL QUARTER OF AN HOUR.

When Edgar closed the front door of the Cavanagh mansion behind himself and Emma, the noise he made was slight, and yet it was heard by ears that were listening for it in the remote recesses of the kitchen.

"The gentlemen are gone," decided Doris, without any hesitation. "They could not move Miss Hermione from her resolves, and I did not think they could. Nothing can move her but fire, and fire there shall be, and that to-night."

Stealing towards the front of the house, she listened. All was quiet. She instantly concluded that the young ladies were in the parlor, and glided back to a certain closet under the stairs, into which she peered with a satisfied air. "Plenty of stuff there," she commented, and shivered slightly as she thought of putting a candle to the combustible pile before her. Shutting the door, she crept to another spot where lay a huge pile of shavings, and again she nodded with satisfaction at the sight. Finally, she went into the shed, and when she came back she walked like one who sees the way clear to her purposes.

"I promised Mr. Huckins I would not start the blaze till after midnight," said she almost audibly, as she passed again towards the front. "He was so afraid if the fire got started early that the neighbors would put it out before any harm was done. But I haven't the nerve to do such a thing with the young ladies up-stairs. They might not get down safely, or I might not have the power to wake them. No, I will fire it now, while they are in the parlor, and trust to its going like tinder, as it will. Won't the young gentlemen thank me, and won't the young ladies do the same, when they get over the shock of being suddenly thrown upon the world."

Chuckling softly to herself, she looked up-stairs and finally ran quietly up. With a woman's thoughtfulness she remembered certain articles which she felt were precious to the young ladies. To gather these together would be the work of a moment, and it would ease her conscience. Going first to Hermione's room, she threw such objects as she considered valuable into a sheet, and tied them up. Then she tossed the bundle thus made out of one of the side windows. Running to Emma's room, she repeated her operations; and letting her own things go, hastened down-stairs and went again into the kitchen. When she reissued it was with a lighted candle in her hand.

Meantime from the poplar walk two eyes were gazing with restless eagerness upon the house. They belonged to Huckins, who, unknown to Etheridge, unknown to Doris even, had returned to Marston for the purpose of watching the development of his deadly game. He had stolen into the garden and was surveying the place, not so much from any expectation of fire at this hour, as because his whole interest was centred in the house and he could not keep his eyes from it.

But suddenly, as he looks, he detects something amiss, and starting forward, with many muttered exclamations, he draws nearer and nearer to the house, which he presently enters by means of the key he draws from his pocket. As he does so, a faint smell of smoke comes to his nostrils, causing him to mutter: "She is three hours too soon; what does she mean by it?"

The door by which he had entered was at the end of a side hall. He found the house dark, but he was so accustomed to it by this time, that he felt no hesitancy as to his steps. He went at first to the sitting-room and looked in; there was no one there. Then he proceeded to the parlor, which was also empty. "Good," thought he, "they are up-stairs"; and he slid with his quiet step to the staircase, up which he went like the ghost or spectre which he had perhaps simulated the night before. There was a door at the top of the first landing, and he had some thoughts of simply locking this, and escaping. But, he said to himself, it would be much more satisfactory to first make sure that the two girls were really above, before he locked them in; so he crept up farther, and finally came to Hermione's room. The door was shut, but from the light which shone through the keyhole (a light which Doris had left there in her haste and trepidation), he judged Hermione to be within, so he softly turned the key that was in the lock, and glided away to Emma's apartment. This was also closed, but there was a light there, also from the same cause, so there being no key visible he drew a heavy piece of furniture across the doorway, and fled back to the stairs. As he reached them, a blinding gust of smoke swept up through the crevices beneath his feet, but he thought he saw his way clearly, and rushed for the landing. But just as he reached it, the door—the door he had intended to close behind him—shut sharply in his face, and he found himself imprisoned. With a shriek, he dashed against it; but it was locked; and just as he staggered upright again from his violent efforts to batter it down, a red-hot flame shot up through a gap in the staircase and played about his feet. He yelled, and dashed up the stairs. If he were to suffer for his own crime, he would at least have companions in his agony. Calling upon Emma and Hermione, he rushed to the piece of furniture with which he had barred the former's apartment, and frantically drew it aside. The door remained shut; there was no agonized one within to force it open the moment the pressure against it was relieved. Stupefied, he staggered away and ran up the twisted staircase to Hermione's room. Perhaps they were here, perhaps they were both here. But all was silent within, and when he had entered and searched the space before him, even beneath and behind the curtains of the bed for its expected occupant, and found no one there, he uttered such a cry as that house had never listened to, not even when it echoed to its master's final yell of rage and despair.

Doris meanwhile was suffering her own punishment below. When she had lighted the three several piles she had prepared, she fled into the front of the house to spread the alarm and insure the safety of her young mistresses. Passing the staircase she had one quick thought of the likelihood there might be of Hermione or Emma dashing up those stairs in an endeavor to save some of their effects, so she quietly locked the door above in order to prevent them. But when she had done this she heard a shriek, and, startled, she was about to unlock it again when a vivid flame shot up between her and the door making any such attempt impossible. Aghast with terror, fearing that by some error of calculation she had shut her young ladies up-stairs after all, she went shrieking their names through the lower rooms and halls, now filling with smoke and lurid with shooting jets of flame. As no response came and she could find no one in any of the rooms, her terror grew to frenzy and she would have dashed up-stairs at the risk of her life. But it was too late; the stairs had already fallen, and the place was one volcano of seething flame.

XXXII.
THE SPECTRE OF THE LABORATORY.

Had Hermione been allowed time to think, she might have drawn back from such a sudden marriage. But Frank, who recognized this possibility, urged her with gentle speed down the street, and never ceased his persuasions till they stood at the minister's door. Mrs. Lothrop, who had a heart for romance, opened it, and seeing the blushing face and somewhat dishevelled appearance of Hermione, she cast one comprehending look at Frank, and drew them in joyfully.

"You are to be married, are you not?" she asked, welcoming the whole four with the gayest of bows. "I congratulate you, dear, and will take you right away to my best room, where you will find your box and everything else you may need. I am so glad you decided to come here instead of having us go to you. It is so pleasant and so friendly and the Doctor does so dread to go out evenings now."

Small chatter is ofttimes our salvation. Under this little lady's fire of bright talk Hermione lost the tragic feelings of months and seemed to awake to the genialities of life. Turning her grand head towards the smiling little woman she let her own happiness shine from the corners of her mouth, and then following the other's lead, allowed herself to be taken to a cosy chintz-furnished room whose home-like aspect struck warm upon her heart and completed the work of her rejuvenation.

Emma, who was close behind her, laughed merrily.

"Such a chrysalis of a bride," cried she. "Where are the wings with which to turn her into a butterfly?"

Mrs. Lothrop showed them a great box, and then left them. Emma, lifting the lid, glanced shyly at Hermione, who blushed scarlet. Such a lovely array of satin, lace, and flowers! To these girls, who had denied themselves everything and been denied everything, it was a glimpse of Paradise. As one beautiful garment after another was taken out, Hermione's head drooped lower in her delight and the love it inspired, till at last the tears came and she wept for a

few minutes unconstrainedly. When this mood had passed, she gave herself up to Emma's eager fingers, and was dressed in her bridal garments.

The clock was striking ten when Frank's impatience was rewarded by the first glimpse of his bride. She came into the room with Emma and Mrs. Lothrop, and her beauty, heightened by her feelings to the utmost, was such as to fill him with triumph and delight.

To Edgar it was a revelation, for always before, he had seen the scar before he did her; but now he was compelled to see her first, for the scar was hidden under fold upon fold of lace.

"No wonder Frank is daft over her," thought he, "if she always looks like this to him."

As for Frank, he bowed with all his soul to the radiant vision, and then, leading her up to Mr. Lothrop, awaited the sacred words which were to make them one. As they were being uttered, strange noises broke out in the street, and the cry of "Fire! fire!" rang out; but if the bride and bridegroom heard the ominous word they did not betray the fact, and the ceremony proceeded. It was soon over, and Frank turned to kiss his wife; but just as Emma advanced with her congratulations, the front door burst open and a neighbor's voice was heard to cry in great excitement:

"The Cavanagh house is burning, and we are all afraid that the girls have perished in the flames."

It was Emma who gave the one shriek that responded to these words. Hermione seemed like one frozen. Edgar, dashing to the door, looked out, and came slowly back.

"Yes, it is burning," said he. "Emma will have to go with you to New York."

"It is a judgment," moaned Hermione, clinging to Frank, who perhaps felt a touch of superstitious awe himself. "It is a judgment upon me for forgetting; for being happy; for accepting a deliverance I should not have desired."

But at these words Frank regained his composure.

"No," corrected he, "it is your deliverance made complete. Without it you might have had compunctions and ideas of returning to a place to which you felt yourself condemned. Now you never can. It is a merciful Providence."

"Let us go and see the old house burn," she whispered. "If it is a funeral pyre of the past, let us watch the dying embers. Perhaps my fears will vanish with them."

He did not refuse her; so Emma relieved her of her veil and threw about her a long cloak, and together they stepped into the street. The glare that struck their faces made them shrink, but they soon overcame the first shock and hastened on.

The town was in a tumult, but they saw nothing save the flaming skeleton of their home, with the gaunt outlines of the poplars shining vividly in the scarlet glow.

As they drew near to it the front of the house fell in, and Hermione, with a shriek, pointed to the corner where the laboratory had been.

"My father! my father! See! see! he is there! He is denouncing me! Look at his lifted arms! It *is* a judgment, it is— —"

Her words trailed off in choking horror. They all looked, and they all saw the figure of an old man writhing against a background of flame. Was it a spectre? Was it the restless ghost of the old professor showing itself for the last time in the place of his greatest sin and suffering? Even Edgar was silent, and Frank refused to say, while the girls, sinking upon their knees with inarticulate moans and prayers, seemed to beg for mercy and cry against this retribution, when suddenly Hermione felt herself clasped in two vigorous arms, and a voice exclaimed in the husky accents of great joy:

"You are here! You are here! You are not burned! O my dear young mistresses, my dear, dear young mistresses!"

Hermione, pushing the weeping Doris back, pointed again towards the toppling structure, and cried:

"Do you see who is there? My father, Doris, my father! See how he beckons and waves, see— —"

Doris, startled, gave a cry in her turn:

"It is Mr. Huckins! O save— —"

But the words were lost in the sudden crash of falling walls. The scene of woe was gone, and the dayspring of hope had risen for the two girls.